D1360329

HE CAN'T HELP IT.
IT'S ALZHEIMER'S

*A Husband and Wife's Battle with Dementia of the
Alzheimer's Type*

Dorothy F. Steele

This book is dedicated to my late husband, Acy Steele Jr.
07/28/1940–12/23/2010

My condolences to Joan Gershman for the loss of her husband, Sidney Gershman. After a twelve year battle, he succumbed to the ravages of Alzheimer's disease. He inspired Joan to create the Alzheimer's Spouse website.

TABLE OF CONTENTS

CHAPTER 1

THE EARLY YEARS

Christmas of 2006

Christmas is close at hand, and 2006 is almost gone. The Christmas tree stands tall, and the lights seem to be dancing as the sound of "Jingle Bell Rock" fills the air. I disappear into the bedroom. I hear the crinkle of the Christmas wrapping paper as I cut each piece and wrap the gifts. I wrap the last one and return to the living room to find Acy sitting in my rocker. He's rummaging through some papers I've been sorting.

"Acy, will you leave my papers alone? You're mixing them up." He continues to shuffle them. I'm not sure he's aware I'm in the room. "Will you please stop? You're mixing the bills with the trash."

Some unknown force appears to drive him.

Firmly I say, "You need to leave them alone. I don't go through your papers."

I sit down at my desktop computer. It's on the other side of the room. He springs to his feet, and in one bound he leaps across the floor. He grabs me by the neck of my blouse and draws his fist back. I'm shocked into submission. My heart pounds in my ears. My gut instinct tells me the way this ends depends on how I respond in the next few seconds.

He's never hit me, and he hesitates now. I take this as a good sign. I glance outside the window, as a cardinal flutters by. He yanks my blouse, jerks me toward him, and shakes his fist in my face. "Look at me!"

I see a face, red and thin lipped from anger. His eyes look glazed and seem to stare as if he's forgotten how to blink. This isn't the first time I've seen this look, but it's the first time he's shown signs of violence.

My eyes drift away, and again he shakes his fist. "I said, look at me!"

Thoughts sprint though my mind. *Should I try to get away? A struggle at this point could end badly.*

His fist is inches from my face, but I decide to focus on his eyes. I search for the man who would never harm me. No words are spoken as our eyes lock. My only hope is that I can look deep enough to find and draw him back. His fist relaxes, and he lowers it slightly. I sit still and try not to provoke him further. I gaze into his eyes as the anger slowly vanishes from his face.

To my relief, as if a switch from within him has been thrown, I see a light in his eyes. He acts as though nothing happened. He lies down on the couch and turns on the TV. In the thirty-one years of our marriage, I've never seen him react this violently.

I'm afraid I might set him off again. At this point, he's quiet and appears unconcerned. It occurs to me that if something serious takes place here, no one will have any idea he has been acting out of character.

Acy retires to the bedroom for the evening. It's too early for me, so I snuggle into my rocker with my laptop and search the Internet for information on sudden violence. I discover the possibility that he might have dementia of the Alzheimer's type. I read that the person afflicted has no control over the violence because Alzheimer's damages the part of the brain that controls emotions. The information I find advises me to have a room ready, should I need to escape. There should be a lock on the door, a phone, and emergency phone numbers in the room. I also discover that the stares he's been giving me the past few years are known as Alzheimer's stares. It's hard to believe our life is about to take this turn. I'm overwhelmed, so I end my research for the night, and I put my laptop away.

It's 11:30 p.m. The day's events make my head spin. Sleep won't come easy tonight. The stillness echoes off the walls. *How has our life come to this?* I wonder. My mind moves back in time and searches for answers.

Life Before Alzheimer's

Acy chose building construction as his profession, and he built my parents' home. I lived in Ohio at the time, and my sister and I met him when we visited Mom and Dad.

When Acy and I were introduced, one name came to mind, Clint Eastwood. He never talked, never smiled, and had a face that showed no emotions. This left me wondering what he had on his mind. He came across as the epitome of the strong, silent type. He strived for independence and didn't believe in marriage.

We felt an immediate attraction. For a twenty-five-year-old divorcée who swore never to marry again and a thirty-four-year-old confirmed bachelor who swore never to marry, it didn't take us long to set a wedding date.

I made the trip back to Ohio to settle my affairs, and Acy made all the arrangements, from blood tests, to the minister.

With Ohio behind me I returned for our nuptials. We stood in front of the minister as he started the ceremony. At this point Acy moved in closer, and I felt the weight of his body bare down on mine. I had trouble supporting him, but we made it through the ceremony. Afterward, Acy became ill and had to lie down.

By evening, he felt better so we continued with the reception. Later, we went on our way to the hotel. He stopped for gas and came back with a bag of goodies. I looked in the bag and spotted a roll of Life Savers.

"LIFESAVERS!" Being me, I ask, "Who do you think will need these tonight, you or me?"

Being Acy, he showed only a slight grin as he continued driving up the road, and he never did say who the Life Savers were for.

The next day, I discovered the Life Savers made it through the night, and I put the roll in a safe, just in case one of us might need them some day. Years later, I found the Life Savers dissolved and stuck to the safe. At that moment I understood the moral of the Life Savers, "If you learn to lean on each other you'll never need your Life Savers."

Acy had developed an alcohol dependency while in the army. I didn't know him during that time of his life, but he explained to me that he had sporadic binges every three or four months.

After we married, he abstained from alcohol. In the course of treatments by several different doctors, it was discovered that the use of alcohol was covering up a more serious problem. While under extensive care by one doctor, he was diagnosed with posttraumatic stress disorder.

During this time, we decided to go into business for ourselves, so we formed our own construction company. Acy's struggle with PTSD eventually left him unable to work productively. He applied and with the help and support of a savvy lawyer he received compensation from the Veteran's Administration.

1992–1994

As I take this journey back in time, I try to remember when Acy's first signs of illness started. There were early signs of dementia. I just didn't know how to recognize them. I knew for several years that something was wrong with Acy, but I was the only one who seemed to notice.

In 1992, Acy decided to add a garage and room onto our home. Since he hadn't worked on anything constructive in years, he approached this project as a hobby. He and some friends put it under roof the first year. Even with help, the job progressed at a slow pace.

I had the opportunity to watch him work in 1993. He had trouble concentrating. He'd determine the measurement for a board, and by the time he walked across the room to cut it, he would forget the measurement. He started writing everything down. His thinking was sluggish, but his skills seemed intact.

In 1994, even though progress was slow, it was steady. Acy found help for the more challenging jobs, while he and I worked on the smaller tasks a few hours at a time. My job was to hand him tools as needed. We enjoyed the companionship, and it brought us closer together. Then he tried to hang a ceiling fan. That should have been a simple job for him, but when he installed the fan, it wouldn't work.

I studied the instructions, and it didn't seem complicated to me. "Why don't we use the instructions? I'll read them, and you do the work."

I looked up from the book to see a look of pure hatred, eyes of stone, a rigid jawline, and an unblinking stare. His eyes seemed to look straight through me. I automatically wondered what I had done. Up until now, we were getting along better than we ever had. We were working in such harmony, we were in sync with each other, and now this.

His eyes of steel focused on mine. He snapped, "I'm not doing that! It won't work!"

"Well, nothing else has worked."

"I'm not going to keep hanging this ceiling fan."

"It won't hurt to try. It's not working the way it is."

"All right. We'll do it." He threatened, "But I'm telling you right now, it better work!"

"I can't promise it'll work, but it's the only chance we have."

He became sullen and refused to talk. I read the instructions one step at a time as he hung the fan. When we finished, he reached for the switch, and I held my breath. He flipped the switch and the light came on. He checked the fan and made sure it worked correctly. Relief washed over me, but we both realized his building skills were compromised.

As evening wore on, I couldn't get the image of his distorted face out of my mind. I was awake all night, trying to understand how love could turn to hate in an instant. The same thought kept going through my mind. *What did I do to cause him to hate me?* I had no idea I had witnessed his first Alzheimer's stare.

Life returned to normal, but I noticed a vague change in Acy. He would withdraw and didn't have much to say for periods of time. He had always been a quiet person but he had no trouble talking to me.

At first his withdrawal periods were infrequent, so I chalked them up to bad moods. He was fifty-three, and I was forty-four. Why would either of us be thinking about Alzheimer's?

In 1994, Acy stopped working on the house. Shortly after, his mother was diagnosed with cancer. He escorted her to the doctor for her appointments and checked on her daily to see if he could do anything to help her. His sisters took care of her personal needs and the domestic chores.

1995

Acy's mother died in 1995. Throughout her illness, Acy spent most of his time at her side. She died at home, and Acy's lack of a reaction baffled me. He appeared to be detached emotionally. As he prepared the house to help the ambulance attendants remove her body, he showed no emotions. His face was vacant, and he never made a sound. Not even a sigh. During the wake and funeral, he didn't talk or cry, and after the funeral was over, he never spoke of it again.

He became the primary caregiver for his eighty-six-year-old father. Acy helped Dad with his physical needs and ran errands for him. His sisters tended to the domestic chores around the house. While Acy handled the doctors' appointments and helped Dad with his medicine, I noticed Acy being uncommonly forgetful. Since there didn't appear to be anything else wrong, I thought it stemmed from his PTSD plus the stress of caring for his father.

A small notebook and pen that fit in his shirt pocket became his constant companion. He used them to keep track of everything he did or needed to do.

1996–1997

In 1996, Acy began having trouble with the small chores around the house, so friends and family finished the remodeling job. Acy stayed on the jobsite and helped with anything he could do.

After the house was finished, Acy's bouts of withdrawal became more frequent. Conversations were sparse, and he never expressed any emotion except anger. When I tried to talk to him about an emotional issue, he would sit quietly and stare into space. He showed no emotional support, leaving me to feel he didn't care. It felt as if he was creating a barrier between us.

In 1996, Acy discovered an article written about the US Department of Defense. They were investigating the relationship between PTSD and Alzheimer's disease. The VA helped complete the investigation. The study found that veterans diagnosed with PTSD were twice as likely as other veterans to develop Alzheimer's disease. Since he was being treated for PTSD, his concern about the connection between the two, prompted him to tuck the article away in his briefcase. Acy didn't share this information with me. I discovered it years later while looking for other papers.

By 1997, he spent most of his time at his dad's. He would leave before daylight and return for lunch and a nap. After his nap, he went back to Dad's. I wouldn't see him again until after 9:00 p.m. That was when he put Dad to bed for the night. Acy would then eat dinner and retire to the bedroom. Days would go by with very few words between us. I took his silence as indifference. I tried to talk to him. I wanted to know what I'd done to make him act that way. His response was always, "It's not you. It's me."

That's one of the oldest lines in the book, I thought.

I found outside activities to stay busy and played a lot of solitaire at home.

1998

I was at Dad's home one day in 1998, and he cornered me. He wanted to talk about Acy. He wanted to know if I had noticed a change in him. I hesitated to discuss Acy with Dad for fear of upsetting him. He wanted to know why Acy spent so much time at his house. He said, "You know, Acy doesn't need to come out here early in the morning. I could use the extra sleep."

"Dad, I have no idea what drives Acy to show up here so early."

With concern written on his face, Dad shook his head and left the room.

Before we could come to terms with this change, Acy changed again. He turned into a roadrunner. He would check on Dad early each morning, and then at 8:00 a.m., he would drive down the road. He would visit with whoever was working at the stores and the gas station. Every day he showed up at the funeral home for coffee with his buddies who worked there. They always had his coffee ready for him. He never stayed long in any one place. From there, he would head home and visit with his cousins along the way. At noon he'd pull into Dad's drive to deliver whatever supplies he had bought for him. Next, he returned home with bags of apples and other fruits. I tried to talk to him about his incessant behavior. "Acy, why are you driving up and down the road?"

"I don't know. I just need to go."

"Why do you visit so much each day?"

"I can't stay in one place for long. I need to go."

I was thankful he settled down in the afternoon and things returned to normal.

1999

In 1999, I questioned my relationship with Acy. I became relentless in my pursuit to understand why his feelings had changed for me. I returned home one day, and he handed me a note. In it, he expressed his love for me and signed the note. He drew a seal on it that read, "My word is my bond." At times, this note was all I had.

I began to accept the change in Acy. When I had doubts about his feelings for me, he seemed to pick up on them, and I would find little love notes he had written and placed where he knew I would see them. It became obvious that his emotions were intact, but he had lost the ability to express them. He found an outlet through writing. I finally understood what he was trying to tell me. It wasn't me. It was him.

As I look back, one my biggest regrets was that I pursued this issue aggressively. If I had known Alzheimer's was preventing him from expressing his feelings, I would have been more understanding.

2000

The first obvious sign of dementia, that I noticed, came in 2000. Every time I would tell him something, he would say someone else had already told him. One day I informed him of some personal information that no one else knew.

"I know," he said.

"How do you know?"

"Someone already told me."

"Who?" I asked.

"I can't remember who."

I suspected he had trouble perceiving what he had heard. I tried to voice my concerns, but he didn't think it was anything serious. Still, I worried.

Around this time, I noticed his sense of smell was changing. I always used ammonia when I did spring cleaning. Acy hated it, and his complaints were intense. This year was different. Suddenly, he didn't seem to notice. I wondered why. I had no idea that losing the ability to smell ammonia is an early sign of Alzheimer's.

2001–2002

In 2001, Acy started staying home more. He spent the morning caring for Dad, and he stayed at home in the afternoon and evening. He returned to Dad's long enough to dress him for bed and see that he was tucked in for the night.

We had been talking about buying a computer, so when Dad kept asking if he could buy us one, Acy finally agreed. Acy had problems learning how to use it. He tried to cover. "I don't want to learn this stuff. I've got better things to do." Before long, he lost interest.

The year 2002 proved a difficult year for us. In the spring, Acy admitted Dad to a nursing home. Acy could no longer care for him. His father died a month later. At the funeral, Acy had trouble containing his grief. After the services, while everyone else was leaving, he collapsed into a chair. It was as if all the pent-up emotions from the past few years had come forth at one time. The funeral procession was delayed, and his buddies from the funeral home surrounded him until he was able to pull himself together. Later that evening, we talked about his emotional outburst. He said he was overwhelmed by his emotions when he realized he would never see Dad again. After that, his ability to express his emotions returned.

That summer, Acy developed a sore on his gums. It looked similar to a picture of a precancerous sore. When I mentioned this to him, I was met with denial.

2003

By 2003, the sore on Acy's gums made it difficult for him to eat. He went to the dentist. The dentist refused to pull his teeth. Acy agreed to see an ear, nose, and throat specialist to check the sore. After tests, the doctor diagnosed oral cancer and made him an appointment with Dr. Horne, an oncologist.

He kept his appointment with Dr. Horne and was told he would need surgery that had to be done at another hospital.

Acy became uncooperative. "Why can't you do it here?"

"Because it's a dangerous operation, and we're not equipped."

"Then why not do radiation?"

"Because it will destroy too many cells and kill your jawbone."

Acy's eyes shifted around the room while he fidgeted in his seat. "How long do I have?"

"It will depend on how long the cancer takes to reach a vital organ," Dr. Horne answered.

Acy sprang to his feet and shouted, "I'm going home! I'll put an end to this!"

Dr. Horne tried but couldn't calm him. He pushed Dr. Horne to one side and bounded toward the door. I could do nothing but follow him.

Acy decided to get another opinion, so a few weeks later, he kept an appointment with another ear, nose, and throat specialist. Dr. Pence explained the treatment and where it would be performed. Acy frowned and rubbed his forehead. He asked questions but kept repeating them. He stood, and then he paced around the room. He refused treatment. While he ranted, the doctor called me aside. He told me to let him know if Acy changed his mind, and he'd call the hospital.

When we returned home, he said he needed time to think. "I want to be left alone and not reminded of the cancer."

For a week he stared at the TV, not really seeing anything. He refused to talk. This was his decision to make. I prepared myself for the worst.

A week went by, and one morning he found me in the kitchen. He stood quietly and with a subdued voice said, "If you want to, you can call the doctor, but wait until after your birthday."

While we tried to celebrate my birthday, we felt smothered by the fog of uncertainty. The next day, I called Dr. Pence, and he helped make the arrangements.

Acy refused to accept the appointment until I found someone to care for his cats. He had rescued several of them from the streets.

During his first appointment, the chief surgeon said it was unusual for smoking to lead to this type of cancer. In case it might have contributed to it, Acy quit smoking.

The chief surgeon explained to Acy that surgery meant a ten-day hospital stay to remove the cancer. The surgery was estimated to take ten hours.

I stayed at a hotel room within walking distance of the hospital. I walked to the hospital the day of the surgery and found Acy in his room. They had delayed his surgery. We sat, talked, and comforted each other. Later, I was thankful for this time together. It was the last time things were normal for us.

While in the ICU, after surgery, he became obsessed with the tubes hanging from his body. He couldn't be reasoned with, and they tied his arms to the bed so he couldn't pull at the tubes. A few days later, they removed the tubes, untied his arms, and moved him to his room.

When the man in the next bed received his meal, Acy got upset because they didn't bring him one. "They aren't giving me anything to eat."

I showed him the feeding tube and explained how it worked. I repeated this to him at every meal.

When I returned from lunch one day, he announced, "I found something to eat."

"What are you talking about?" I asked.

He pointed to an empty can. He told me the nurse had left the cans on the table. He said that after the nurse walked out the door, he picked one up and drank it. I examined the cans and found they held the formula for his feeding tube. I reported this to the assisting doctor.

He laughed and said, "It won't hurt him, but it may give him an upset stomach."

Thank goodness he didn't react to the formula.

Acy continued to fuss about not having a tray at mealtime, so they removed the feeding tube and put him on a liquid diet. When the tray arrived, he refused to eat. I tried to persuade him to eat something. He yelled, "I don't want anything. Now leave me alone!"

As I turned and walked out the door, I fought the urge to lash out at him. *Maybe things will be better tomorrow*, I thought.

The next day, he still refused to eat. I tried to explain the situation to him. Without the feeding tube, he needed to eat to receive nourishment. At the end of the day, I returned to the hotel. I felt frustrated and defeated.

The following morning, I found him sitting on the bed fully dressed. The doctor had released him two days early, and he was ready to go home.

How on earth am I going to persuade him to eat? His teeth were removed during surgery, and at the cancer site, part of his hip bone had replaced his jawbone. Part of his gums were removed, and skin had been taken from his stomach to make a skin graft over the area where the gums once were. They had slit his throat to remove his lymph nodes.

After we arrived home and settled in, I realized I had the advantage of knowing what foods he liked and disliked. He loved chicken noodle soup with crackers soaking in it, and he always drank his milk. Instead of gelatin, I gave him chocolate pudding. Once he started eating, I worked out a diet for him.

Although his physical recovery at home went smoothly, his mental health was fragile. He wore his pajamas day and night. He wore them when he mowed the grass, but he wore street clothes if he went to town. One day when I returned home from shopping, he wanted to tell me something, but he was embarrassed.

"What's wrong?" I asked.

"I went to the store in my pajamas."

Time passed, and this ceased to be a big deal for him. Sometimes he changed clothes, and other times he didn't.

I always tried to stop him on his way out. "Acy, you need to change your clothes when you go down the road."

He'd continue toward the truck. "I don't need to. No one else will know the difference."

People who noticed this, later commented they thought it odd, but they didn't realize the seriousness of the situation.

2004

In 2004, Acy had a hard time accepting that his mental recall wasn't getting better. Frequently, he threatened suicide. He was still highly functional. We believed his problems were from having surgery and hoped they'd pass. He healed physically, but his mental health remained vulnerable.

My health issues that year brought new problems to light for Acy. During a colonoscopy, my blood pressure kept dropping. This led to a battery of tests on my heart, and they wanted me to do an angiogram.

During the procedure, my heart stopped, and they resuscitated me. The doctor proceeded with the test. Afterward, I was told I would be transported to an out-of-state hospital for surgery to place stents in my heart.

The doctor told the staff he would find my husband and talk to him. I became adamant. "He can't go with me. He needs to go home."

I heard the doctor tell someone nearby, "After all she's going through, and she's worrying about her husband."

He didn't understand. The last thing I needed was to worry about Acy following the ambulance. I needed to know he was safe at home, where he could make arrangements for my return.

The doctor put me in a room to wait for an ambulance. Acy appeared and sat down. He seemed lost and despondent. We started talking, and I gave him instructions on things that needed to be done while I was gone. I saw tears sliding down his face. The only time I had seen him cry was at Dad's funeral, and I wasn't sure how to respond. I waited silently. I needed to keep a cool head since no other part of me seemed to be working.

After his tears were spent, he sat quietly. I suggested he go home and find someone to drive me home after my procedure. Since we lived in a small town and the people at the funeral home were always willing to help, I told him to seek their assistance in finding someone to make the long drive and bring me back home.

"You need to leave now so you have time to do these things," I told him. I worried it would add to his anxiety if he saw me leave first.

The ambulance arrived, and four hours later, we reached the hospital. I settled in my room, and Dr.

Chapman came in to talk to me. I had surgery the following morning.

Even though Acy had been given phone numbers to call, I didn't hear from him. I called him the night I arrived at the hospital and the next day to let him know everything went well and when I'd be discharged.

"I tried to call but couldn't figure out how to work the menus," he said. "Fifteen minutes after I arrived home from the hospital, I found someone to bring you home. I'll ride with him."

Acy and his driver arrived, and we were soon on our way home. After a long trip, I was thankful to be in my own house. We relaxed on the couch, and Acy talked about what this experience had been like for him.

"None of the numbers the hospital gave me were helpful. Every time I dialed one, I either had to wade through menus or I'd be referred to another number. You have no idea how it felt not knowing what was going on or if you were all right."

He spoke of our departure at the hospital. "You made me leave." His voice trembled. "I wanted to stay with you as long as I could. I went to the truck and cried. I didn't know if I would ever see you again."

I took his hand in mine. "I'm sorry." I shared his anguish. "I thought I was making it easier for you."

We continued to talk. I questioned him to find out if he had been eating properly while I was gone. He said his sister used the pureed food I had frozen to prepare his meals. He squeezed my hand and said, "I'm sure glad you're home."

How sweet, I thought. "I'm glad I'm home too."

Then I heard, "My food is almost gone."

I laughed. "Time to put on my apron."

2005

The year 2005 found us adjusting to our new handicaps. The past couple of years had brought us closer together. Acy quit saying things he knew would upset me, and he no longer mentioned suicide. He went out of his way to care for me.

We decided to buy a car. He had always handled the details. This time, he sent me by myself. I found a car I liked and worked out the purchase agreement.

At first I didn't understand why he no longer wanted to be the one to make these decisions. After some observation, I realized that he became confused when the conversations were complex.

When it came time, he insisted I take the car to be serviced. He said I needed to learn to do this myself. I think he realized before I did that things were getting worse.

2006

I noticed Acy's memory loss becoming serious in 2006, but he refused to seek help.

In the spring, he encouraged me to learn how to use his lawn tractor. The tractor was too big and complicated for me, so he told me to pick one out that suited me. After a few days of shopping, I found one that was easier to operate and called him from the dealership. He wanted to pick it up in his truck. I waited for him at the dealership.

He was late, so I decided to look for him. Even though he had driven this route many times over the years, I found him at an intersection as he took a wrong turn. I followed him, blew my horn, and motioned for him to stop. He followed me back to the dealership, and we purchased the tractor.

As I learned how to use my tractor, he mowed the more difficult sections. This gave me time to learn how to maneuver the tractor. My mowing wasn't prefect, but it satisfied me.

One day, while we were mowing, he pulled up beside me in the yard. With a playful sparkle in his eyes, he challenged me. "Hey Faye, let's go racing."

With a smile, I accepted the challenge. "You got it."

We lined up side by side, and he yelled, "We're off!"

Sprint Cup material we're not. We raced down the yard on our tractors, and I realized the neighbors were watching. It was too late to wonder what they thought. He won the race by a front tire.

"That's because your tires are bigger," I told him.

He grinned and accepted victory with modesty.

Summer turned to fall and fall to winter. He had more good days than bad ones. He only ventured out in public on his good days. On these days, he could function on most levels, and no one suspected he was ill. Things were about to change.

About a month ago, while we relaxed in the living room, he shook his fist at me. At first I ignored him. He continued to do this more often as time passed. I tried to find out what brought this on. "Why have you started shaking your fist at me?"

"I don't do that."

"Yes, you do."

"You don't know what you're talking about."

"You've shaken your fist at me several times."

"It's just your imagination," he answered.

His denial caused me to become even more concerned.

As dawn breaks, daylight interrupts my thoughts. I've been reminiscing all night, and searching the past for answers. I try to understand what brought on Acy's violent reaction to my confrontation over the papers, yesterday. I can see how his melt down yesterday has been a long time coming. Thinking his problems stemmed from PTSD and his surgery made me slow to understand what was going on. I wonder if I could have prevented the confrontation if I had known the signs of Alzheimer's disease.

As the dawn rises, so does Acy. He's unusually quiet. After breakfast, his mood changes, and he wants to argue. *I don't think so.* "I'll never argue with you again," I say, but he doesn't respond.

For as long as I have known Acy, he's loved to argue, and I have always obliged him. Not anymore. Throughout the day, he continues to be argumentative. When he tries to argue, I ignore him, and without encouragement, the day passes without incident. By the end of the day, I'm ready for a good night's sleep, and so is he.

From this moment on, I will keep a record of the changes I see in him.

CHAPTER 2

2007

Hernia Surgery

So far, this year has been peaceful and uneventful. We've found an interesting hobby. Acy's going through his childhood pictures and picking out some for me to Photoshop. We spend hours each day working with his pictures. With the help of my *Photoshop Elements For Dummies*, I restore them and even add color to a few of the black and whites. He wants to put them in the local paper, so I send them in by e-mail for him. With his pictures and my book, we can get things done. We're happy and content, and life is good.

This is a quiet and peaceful time, with nothing important on our agenda. I start thinking about my much needed surgery. After three years, I decide it's time to have my hernia repaired. It'll be done in out-patient surgery. The trip to the hospital is over an hour long, so we leave before daylight.

Due to an emergency, my surgery is delayed. It's late but they are going ahead with surgery. It's dark outside by the time I'm returned to my room. I'm somewhat sedated, but they are releasing me. The aide helps me dress and tells Acy, "She isn't steady on her feet. She'll need your help when you get home."

We arrive home, and as soon as we walk through the door, he announces, "I haven't had anything to eat all day."

"I haven't either," I reply. I try to put him a meal together, but he won't hush.

"Well, hurry up and fix me something."

"I'm trying."

"I'm weak from hunger."

"I'm almost finished."

"You shouldn't have kept me out all day." He sits down in his chair and starts to sulk.

I prepare his dinner, but my head is too foggy to operate the microwave. I set the plate on the table and go to bed. The next day, he's still ranting. "You went to bed last night, and I had to eat my supper cold!"

I wasn't aware he had forgotten how to use the microwave. I find it hard to sympathize with him.

He's acting like a child who is only aware of his own needs. I'm now looking at my man-child.

The doctor gave me instructions with strict limits about what I'm allowed to do because of the surgery. He tells me not to drive for a month. When the time comes for my follow-up at the doctor's office, I find someone else to take me. From now on, Acy's driving is limited to areas closer to home.

Afrin Obsession

It's spring, and Acy's allergies are bothering him. Afrin has always been his standby for allergy flare-ups. There's no surprise when he brings a bottle home, but I notice more than a few empty bottles in a short time. It's obvious he's obsessed with shooting it up his nose.

"Are you sure you should be using so much?"

He becomes indignant and replies, "I'm not a child. I know what I'm doing."

I want no part of this, so I refuse to buy him any. He goes to different stores and buys several bottles. When he returns, he lines them all up on the coffee table. He leaves the room and comes back with a pair of scissors. Next he opens a new bottle of Afrin. He uses the scissors to cut off the bottle's tip.

"Why did you do that?"

"Because the hole is too small. There's not enough coming out of the tip." He proceeds and doesn't stop until he has shot all the Afrin up his nose.

I try to convince him that's too much at one time.

"I don't care," he says. "I'm going to the store and buy every bottle of Afrin on the shelf."

He leaves and returns with ten bottles of Afrin. I have no idea what to do, but I know I need to do something. On the verge of panic, I come up with a plan.

First I work on regaining his trust. Before I go to the store, I ask, "Do you need any Afrin?"

"Yes."

"OK. I'll pick you up some while I'm out." I also buy several large bottles of saline spray. When I return home, I carry the saline and Afrin into the house.

"I'll go get the rest of the packages," he says.

"Thank you, dear."

He heads for the car, and I take a bottle of saline to the kitchen. I alter the tip and have it ready to use at a moment's notice. He finishes and sits down on the couch. I give him the Afrin, and he smiles and gives me a thumbs-up. "Thank you, Faye baby." I'm not sure whether he wants to remove the seal himself. I watch as he tries to open the package.

With all the compassion I can muster, I say, "That's a little hard to remove. Let me do that for you."

"OK," he says with a sigh of relief.

He uses the Afrin while I wait. He stands up and disappears into the bathroom. This is my best chance. I grab the bottle and remove the top, while I run to the kitchen sink. I empty the bottle and refill it with the saline. Using an ink pen, I put an X on the bottom of the Afrin bottle. I hurry to put it back where he left it.

He returns from the bathroom and hands me his other bottles. "Will you open these for me?"

I take them to the kitchen, open them, and switch the Afrin and saline before I give them back to him. While he sleeps, I search the medicine cabinet and replace any Afrin I find. I continue to mark the bottoms in case one finds its way into the house without me knowing. I save the empty ones and refill them with saline. I do this for two weeks.

"This isn't working anymore," he says. He decides the Afrin doesn't help and stops using it.

This incident has made me aware that I need to find someone to help us.

My Certificate of Deposit

Today starts out as a normal day. My CD has matured, and I'm going to the bank to reinvest it. We have separate CDs with both our names on them. I know this one's mine because it's the smaller of the two. At the bank I want to reinvest the CD, and they ask for a current driver's license photo of Acy. I decide to put the money in our checking account until I talk to him.

When I arrive home, I find Acy in the living room. I tell him, "The bank wants a copy of your driver's license."

He rages, "Damn that bank! They don't have any right to my license!"

"They need it for identity purposes."

"Well, they won't get my license."

"All they want is a copy so they can identify you."

"They're not getting it! I'm going to withdraw my money!"

"That's my CD," I say.

"That's not your CD! Most of that money is mine."

He's never acted this way before, and I don't know how to respond. He proceeds to the bathroom to wash and dress for his trip to the bank.

I need to put a stop to this. "If you want me to, I'll go get the money."

He hesitates and thinks about it. "All right, but don't take too long."

This has bought me some time. I drive to the bank and ask for a certified check for most of the money in the account. I leave enough to keep the account open and pay bills. I have no idea what to do now.

I return home to face the consequences. I know if I don't stand up to him, he will destroy us financially. As I enter the house, I think, *I'm about to get my ass whipped.* I don't see him, so I hide the check. I find him in the bedroom watching the TV.

"Did you get everything straightened out at the bank?"

"Yes." I'm not about to volunteer any information.

He seems satisfied and goes back to watching the TV. I'm left with the impression he remembers the meltdown but not the details. This is good news for me.

The next morning, as we sit in the living room, he asks about the amount of the CD. When I tell him, he becomes concerned. "My CD is supposed to have more money than that."

"Your CD does. That was my CD."

"Oh, well, I don't want your money."

This ends the dispute for now.

That afternoon, I put the money back into the account. I keep some of it in cash, in case I need to pacify him. I make a mental note to move the remaining amount of the CD into another account in my name only.

Late that evening, he naps, and I swipe his billfold from the nightstand drawer. I hustle back to the living room. I remove his driver's license from his billfold and make several copies to have on hand should I need them. I check on him. He's still asleep, so I replace the billfold.

Aricept

During my June appointment with my general physician, Dr. Trent, I mention Acy's behavior. She promises to talk to him at his next appointment.

Acy keeps his appointment with Dr. Trent. She calls me from her office and asks how she can help.

"All you need to do is talk to him for a few minutes," I tell her. "Just talk to him."

In about ten minutes, she calls back. Concern fills her voice. "I tried to talk to him. He's totally confused and shows signs of Alzheimer's." My greatest fear has been confirmed.

While anticipating his return home, I realize I need to go with him to his appointments in the future. This is a step toward losing his independence and freedom. I'm sure there will be more to come. One of the hardest jobs for me as a caregiver is to know when he can no longer function at certain levels. I'm finding out that people afflicted by Alzheimer's don't lose the knack of doing things all at one time. They lose their abilities at their own pace, and it's up to the caregivers to decide when to relieve them of their responsibilities.

Acy arrives home with a prescription for Aricept. He takes a pill at 9:00 p.m.

The next morning, he finds me in the kitchen with a fresh pot of coffee. I pour him a cup, but he refuses to sit down. He sips his coffee, then he starts pacing the floor. He keeps glancing at the clock.

"What's wrong?" I ask.

He's obsessing about a family feud with the former owner of the house down the road. "I'm going to shoot the windows out of their house," he announces. "Why don't you go to Walmart and buy me a slingshot?"

"Acy, you can't do that. Someone else lives in that house now."

"They don't own it," he says.

"Yes, they do."

"You're wrong!" he says. "If you won't help me, I'll go to Walmart myself."

He leaves and returns with a CO_2-powered BB pistol. He starts to load it. I try to stop him. "You can't do that. Someone could get hurt."

He continues to load the pistol. I know I'm breaking rule number one: never argue with an Alzheimer's patient. I don't know what else to do. He's on the path to destroying our future. He could end up in jail, or our neighbor could have a handgun or rifle. I envision myself on the street without a home or husband.

I try to reason with him. "Your father and grandfather settled this feud many years ago. It's not your fight."

"Now you're talking about my family!"

Since he's related to Devil Anse Hatfield, I know how this could end. "I'm trying to get you to understand that your father, out of respect for his father, decided to not pursue this vendetta. You need to respect his decision and drop this."

He's beyond listening to me, and he has the BB pistol loaded. He heads toward the door. "BBs can't be traced. No one will ever know it was me."

"You can't pull this off. Everyone will know it was you."

"I'll get Curly to do it for me. He owes me a favor."

Curly is a close friend of Acy's and someone I always thought would do anything for him. The threat is real. I'm out of words of wisdom. He's about to see something he's never seen before.

The past few years of pent-up frustration comes pouring out, and for the first time since I have known him, I scream, "I hate you!"

He turns and starts toward me. In a flash, I'm out of my chair and down the hall. I slam the bedroom door. I lock it and sit down on the bed. My heart beats in my ears. It feels as if a thousand pounds rest on my chest, and I shake like a can of paint on a paint shaker. I watch the doorknob move and hear it rattle.

It's hump day, and the straw lies heavy on my back. I feel a scream rise in my throat. The earth-shattering sound of my voice continues nonstop. The doorknob stops moving, and the screaming ceases. All is quiet. I go to the bedroom door and ease it open. Where he's gone, God only knows. My first sensation is relief all the way to my toes. I go to the living room, sit, and wait for his return. Waiting gives me time to reflect on what has happened.

I lost control. I wasn't prepared for the way his actions could destroy my life. I love Acy with all my heart, so why would I say I hated him? My mind stops racing, and my thoughts begin to clear. I realize Alzheimer's is not only affecting Acy's life, but I will also suffer the consequences of his actions. I understand now. I don't hate Acy. I hate Alzheimer's and what it's doing to him. I hate what it's doing to me, through him. I add, telling Acy I hate him, to my list of many reasons to feel guilty.

Two hours pass, and the front door opens. I brace myself for whatever is to come. He walks past me on his way to the kitchen, but he doesn't speak. He pulls canned food from the bags he's carrying and puts the cans in the pantry.

Knowing all his food has to be pureed, I ask, "Do you want me to prepare you something?"

"No, I can feed myself."

"All right," I say.

With a look of determination on his face, he heads to the bedroom. I check on him. He's sitting on the bed and putting his billfold in the nightstand. I return to the living room, but before I can sit down, I hear a gunshot blast from the bedroom.

I rush back to find him holding his shotgun out the window. He's killed a bird at one of my bird feeders. As he leaves to dispose of it, I realize it's one of the new arrivals.

A few days ago, a flock of pigeons flew in behind the house. They had never been here before. A hawk was circling, and the pigeons were using the house for a place to hide. After the hawk left, I scared them away because Acy hates pigeons. One stood out because of his unique shades of color. He had glittering blue and pink feathers. He stood firmly on a rock, six feet from the back door. Every day he returned. No matter what I did, he refused to leave. I started talking to him. He kept looking at me, turning his head and blinking his eyes as if he understood. I was spellbound by his beauty. He wasn't afraid and acted as if he knew me. Because of me, he's lost his life.

With a shotgun in one hand and the bird in the other, Acy crosses the road. The neighbors are sitting on the porch, and one of them appears upset. The others tell her to stay out of it.

I sit in my living room and wonder what he'll do next. He returns and heads for the bedroom. I follow and reach the door in time to see him take aim out the window. Guilt consumes me. Because of me, the birds and squirrels feel this is a safe place to eat. I've fed them for years, and now I'm crushed. I can't stand the thought of him killing another one just because he's angry at me.

"Acy, please don't shot any more birds!" I beg.

He throws his head back, but his laugh is silent. Shivers run through me.

"They haven't done anything to you. Please, stop!" There is no response, so I try to distract him. "Why don't you and I go to the living room?"

He doesn't answer. He continues to take aim. What to do escapes me. I know not to try to take the gun. I go back to the living room and sit down. I understand that his ability to reason is damaged, but I try to think of a way to reach him. I look up as he walks down the hall without the gun. I breathe a sigh of relief and thank God. He's withdrawn and indifferent. I don't dare speak for fear of what he may do next. Things remain calm and seem normal. Evening turns into night.

The next morning, I tell him, "I need to go to Walmart today."

He responds, "Well, where's Walmart?"

He had no trouble finding the store yesterday when he bought the BB pistol. I wonder how I am going to get through this illness with him.

When I return from Walmart, he wants to go to the bank and withdraw our savings to buy a Cadillac. I know his driving days are numbered. "Since you have Alzheimer's, don't you think we should talk about this?"

"No, I don't have Alzheimer's," he says. "The doctor's wrong."

I refuse to go with him, so he drops the subject.

It's been two days since the altercation over our neighbors' house, and he still refuses my offer to prepare him a meal.

Once again, I ask, "Do you want me to fix you something to eat?"

"OK," he says.

He eats two servings of everything. After he eats, he tells me he visited Curly.

Knowing Acy went there to seek his help in shooting out the neighbors' windows, I tell myself to stay calm. "What was he up to?"

"Oh, he was celebrating his birthday with his family."

I assume Acy didn't get the opportunity to ask for his help.

He calls me over to the pantry and shows me the food he bought. I see typical food for a fishing trip, cans of Vienna sausage, pork and beans, lunch meat, and crackers.

"Can you use any of this?" he asks.

"I don't know."

"You can have any of it you want." This is his attempt at a peace offering.

"Thanks. I may be able to use some of it." I'm leery of having a conversation with him.

The BB pistol hasn't been mentioned, and I haven't seen it for a few days. Today, I see him search through his cabinet. He looks inside a brown bag. I watch out of the corner of my eye as he pulls out the pistol. He puts it back and leaves.

I wait a couple days for him to forget. I go to the cabinet and open the bag. First I find a huge jug of BBs. There is a box of twenty-five CO_2 cylinders. Last is the pistol and instructions. I take the bag and replace it with another one so he doesn't notice an empty space. I throw the BBs in the trash. I read the instructions and warnings, and learn to discharge the cylinders. Each evening, after he retires to the bedroom to watch TV, I go to the other end of the house. I get the pistol and lock myself in the half bath. The bathroom window faces a mountain. I hold the pistol out the window. I dry fire the pistol to discharge the cylinders and hope the TV distorts the sound. I only do one cylinder at a time. I discharge more on the days he goes out. I decide to bury the cylinders as I empty them. I need more time to figure out how to dispose of the pistol. In the meantime, I lock it in a safe.

Things could have been much worse. I'll always remember the little bird whose life was sacrificed for mine. Even though this evil disease drove his actions, a part of me resents Acy for shooting him.

I become worried about my safety. I place money in an envelope and pin it inside a curtain, where I can easily reach it if I need to escape quickly.

While I dispose of the cylinders, Acy has an agenda of his own.

When he retired, he gave away and loaned a lot of his tools. Now, he goes to these people and gets his tools back.

"Why are you doing this?"

He anxiously replies, "I might need to go back to work. Do you understand?"

I want him to stay calm, so I simply nod my head. In reality, I understand nothing.

He remembers a receptacle I wanted that was never put in the electrical switch box. He decides to do this now.

I tell him, "I don't need that receptacle anymore."

"You think I can't do this. I'll do it while you're at the store!"

After he goes to bed that night, I take wire cutters and cut the wire at floor level.

The next morning, he looks for the wire. He appears confused, closes the door to the switch box, and leaves.

On another day, he's gone again. I have no idea where to find him. When he returns, he's all smiles, and he gives me a hug. He shows me his new purchase. It's a bottle of Viagra.

Oh crap! I can't believe what I'm seeing. This is the last thing on my mind.

"What have you been up to?" I ask. I'm glad to see him smile about something.

"I've been to see Dr. Cline."

Acy wants us to make up. He gives me the pills and another hug. He disappears into the bathroom to shower. By the time he returns, he's forgotten the pills. The next day, I throw them away.

A few days later, I hear Acy yelling in his sleep, and he won't turn off his light.

"Why do you leave the light on?"

"Because someone else is using it," he replies.

I never ask again.

Up until now, these manic episodes have been infrequent. I need to figure out what has sparked all these events in the past two weeks. I can think of only one change in his routine. He takes his new medicine, Aricept, at night. By morning, he's so hyper, he grabs his truck keys, gets in his truck, and hits the road without saying where he's going. Meanwhile, I'm trying to get him to cut back on his driving.

He's calm and his old self by evening, before he takes the pill. It's the only time we can have a rational conversation. This evening, I decide to talk to him. "Since you started taking Aricept, I've noticed you yell in your sleep."

"It causes me to have bad thoughts," he informs me.

I don't ask him to tell me about the thoughts. I'm afraid if he dwells on them, he might act on them.

A week passes, and he settles down.

"You seem calmer."

"I quit taking the Aricept," he says.

We talk about what has transpired the past few weeks. He can't remember any of the things he did. He appears calm, so I ask if he really wants a Cadillac. He says no, and he has no memory of ever wanting one. He remembers the high-powered BB pistol but can't remember what he did with it. I decide it's best not to mention the Viagra. One thing is for sure. I'm not going to ask him what he wanted. I can see now that Alzheimer's has moved into our bedroom.

At Acy's next doctor's appointment, Dr. Trent asks about the Aricept. I tell her he quit taking it because we thought he might be having a reaction to it. I inform her, we had the biggest fight of our marriage. I explain that Acy has always been an aggressive man, and the Aricept seemed to make him hyper. It caused him to act on his aggressive feelings. When he stopped taking it, he calmed down and quit acting out every day. She wants to give him half a pill a day. Since Acy's functional and hasn't been declared incompetent, this is out of my hands.

"You can give him what you want, and he can take what he wants, but I don't have to stay around to watch the results," I say.

She decides not to write the prescription. In all fairness, I didn't give her any of the details about the fight.

We leave the office, and as soon as we're in the car, he says, "Will you take me to Walmart to get a slingshot?"

My first thought is, *He isn't as forgetful as one would think. He must be having a good day. Even without details, he knew what fight I was talking about.*

With my blood starting to boil, I speak calmly but firmly. "No, and if you continue to act this way, I won't help you with your medicine."

He sits quietly the rest of the way home.

When we return home, as instructed, I divide the remaining pills in half. A few days later, I notice they're gone.

"I wonder where your pills are."

"I threw them away," he says.

Driving

Acy cuts back on his driving. He's taking fewer trips in his trucks. He continues to go out on his good days. No one knows about his bad days but me, Dr.

Trent, and the pharmacist. It's a matter of time before his driving must stop. The problem is not that he can't drive. He can. I need guidance to help me with the driving issue. I search the Internet and find an article on the Hartford Insurance website that gives guidelines for driving and Alzheimer's. The company recommends slowly taking over the driving jobs before the ability to drive is lost. I decide to follow this course. He now puts gas in my car and takes his trucks out once a week. Each trip is less than a mile. Maybe cutting back on his need to drive will ease the transition. At times I ride with him so I can monitor his driving. So far, he shows no sign of his skills deteriorating. I hope I can pull off the slow decline in driving before he loses them.

We decide to take an hour-long trip into the city. We stop to eat, and when we finish, I maneuver the car back into the street. From across the seat, I hear, "You sure are a good driver."

"Thank you," I say and laugh. While I've been monitoring his driving, he's been monitoring mine.

Shaving

Acy continues to lose ground. After he shaves today, he finishes and puts his razor on the charger. He leaves it running.

"Acy, you're supposed to turn off the razor."

He's belligerent. "I know what I'm doing. I've been shaving for years."

I listen to it run, sitting in the tray, for two hours. Eventually, he turns it off. Thank goodness it still works. I decide he needs my help.

The next day, I offer to help him, and he accepts. He's dissatisfied with the way I've shaved him.

"You missed some spots," he claims. "Let me have the razor."

He runs it over these "spots," and before I can stop him, he runs it up the back of his head.

"Stop!" I shout. "You're cutting your hair!"

I can't tell if he's ignoring me or in a trance. A fight ensues as I try but can't pry the razor from his hand. I can only stand and watch as he continues to clip his hair. I think, *He can't help it. It's Alzheimer's.* He gets tired and quits. There he sits. His head is shaved up one side and around his ear. My mind is having trouble grasping what my eyes see. Thank goodness he always wears a cap when he goes out.

Spitting

I notice Acy's spitting into his handkerchief. "What's the matter?" I ask.

"I need something to spit in."

I give him a yogurt cup and lid. He keeps one with him at all times. He washes it out and makes sure it's always clean. He carries one with him when he goes out, and people want to know if he chews tobacco. The answer is always, "No, and he never has."

I have no idea how to explain his spitting. I worry about his oral cancer returning, so I make an appointment with Dr. Pence. He orders a full-body scan. The scan shows no cancer in his body, and the doctor declares him cancer free. It does show a small aortic aneurysm. While getting the scan done, I discover there's one for people thought to have Alzheimer's disease.

Dr. Pence suggests tests on a regular basis to watch the aneurysm. I ask him if he thinks Acy might benefit from the scan for Alzheimer's. He doesn't think Acy shows any symptoms of Alzheimer's and says he doesn't qualify for this scan.

After some research, I find that spitting is a symptom of Alzheimer's. I read this happens to some, as they lose the ability to swallow. As his caregiver, it's important for me to search for a well-informed doctor.

Doctor's Appointment

Acy wants to drive to Dr. Trent's office for his appointment. I hesitate, but since I'm going with him, this is an opportunity to monitor his driving. He stops for all the red lights and stop signs. He navigates well and stays on his side of the road. He still understands the signals and drives a proper distance from the vehicle in front of him. He never goes over the speed limit, and he remembers the route to the doctor's office. If this had been a test for a driver's license, I believe he would have passed.

At Dr. Trent's office, Acy and I have a long discussion with Dr. Trent about the aortic aneurysm, and we decide there are to be no tests or treatments to extend his life. I believe this will be easier said than done. It's difficult to let go when life support is offered to keep someone alive. It's hard to tell who's playing God—the person offering the support or the person who refuses it. As for me, Acy has already stated his wishes. I must learn to put my feelings aside and accept his choices.

We discuss the trouble Acy is having answering the phone. Several times, people have told me they called when I wasn't home and left messages with him. There are times he can't understand what the callers want or can't remember them. I don't know if he can't or won't write me a note. All I know is, I'm not receiving important information. It's decided that all the telephone ringers should be turned off when I'm not home. That way, messages can be recorded. He can still make a call if he wants to.

I tell Dr. Trent that Acy's problems with social gatherings have accelerated. They have always made him anxious due to his PTSD, but he tires easily now and becomes confused when he's in a group. This stresses both of us. She suggests it may be best for us to avoid these types of gatherings. From now on, I will plan something simple that both of us can enjoy for celebrations.

We leave and start down the hall. I remember something I want to tell Dr. Trent. I step back into the office. Acy waits in the doorway. While talking she mentions it may be time to fill out a do not resuscitate form. I tell her I'll discuss this with Acy.

On the way home, we discuss the fact that he's starting to lose his memory of things in the past. I try to console him by telling him I will be there. I will be his memory.

A new day dawns, and as it progresses, I can see it's a good day for Acy. His thinking is clear, and we're able to have a logical conversation. I decide it's time for a talk. We start talking about keeping people alive by artificial means. He's told me through the years that he doesn't believe in life support if there is no hope for a recovery. I need to see if he still feels the same way.

"If you needed a feeding tube, would you want one?" I ask.

"Not if there isn't any hope," he answers.

"If you needed one today, would you accept it?"

"No." He rethinks and then says, "I don't think I'm that sick."

I respect his decision. For now, I won't be pursuing a do not resuscitate form.

Outside Chores

It's August, and I've done all the mowing this season. Acy hasn't shown any interest in mowing grass, until today. I hear his lawn tractor and look out the window. I see him mowing his sister's yard. A few minutes later, I notice things are quiet. He comes to the door and wants to know if I can help him. I go with him and find his tractor on a slope. It's in a bind, and he can't get it to climb the slope. His sister tells me her daughter called Alan, Acy's friend. They are waiting for him to arrive and help. I've helped Acy out of this predicament a few other times. While they wait, Acy and I push the tractor to a flat spot. He finishes mowing, but this is his last mowing job. As he continues to lose his ability to do his chores, I find myself picking up the slack.

Summer comes to an end, and it's time to change the oil in my tractor. Even though it hasn't been used, Acy changes the oil and greases his tractor. In the meantime, here I stand, a fifty-eight-year-old woman studying the instruction book, and for the first time, I'm struggling to bring forth my mechanical abilities. I follow the instructions to the letter and find myself changing and greasing my tractor.

CHAPTER 3

2008: PART ONE

I Find Support

I search the Internet for information about Alzheimer's disease, and I buy half a dozen books. The lack of awareness I find in my search disappoints me. What's lacking is the human side of this disease. I see very little that addresses what it's like to constantly live and care for someone with dementia. At this time, it's difficult to gain insight about the turmoil a caregiver faces each day and night during this Alzheimer's journey.

I discover a website, TheAlzheimerSpouse.com, founded by Joan Gershman. Her husband is afflicted with Alzheimer's. Along with her blogs, she offers many places where people can find help. After a period of time, lurking on the message board, I decide this is where I belong. I join, and the site becomes my saving grace.

The website is for husbands and wives only. Members come to receive support and discuss problems caused by Alzheimer's. It doesn't take long to feel like part of the family. Advice, ideas, and opinions flow among us. One can come here to vent and cry. We talk about our deepest thoughts and feelings that are uncomfortable to talk about with others. We don't judge. We comfort each other and listen with our hearts while adjusting to our new lives. For those of us who belong, this site has become known as "Joan's Place." The group owes her a debt of gratitude.

What Time is it?

Acy's having trouble with the clocks. He doesn't have a problem in the morning, but in the afternoon he becomes confused. He disregards the short hand and thinks the long hand represents the hour.

He eats lunch at noon. A short time later he wants to know, "Faye, when are you going to fix supper?"

"What time is it?" I ask.

"It's five o'clock."

It's actually 2:25 p.m., and the long hand is on the five. I prepare a snack for him.

The clock strikes three and he notices the long hand on the twelve. "That clock jumped back to twelve. You need to buy some clocks. These don't work anymore."

"OK, I'll do that the next time I go shopping."

It's evening, and he goes to the bedroom around five o'clock. I decide to check on him. The time has been changed on the clock. I notice he's trying to take it apart.

"Why are you doing that?" I ask.

"I want to remove this stub." He points to the little hand. "It confuses me."

"Well, I need it. Why don't we leave it on there?"

"OK, if it makes you happy," he says.

I shop and buy a variety of clocks. I return home and head for the bedroom. I set a digital clock by the TV on the chest.

Acy grows fond of this clock. Each night, he retires early to the bedroom, and watches the clock instead of the TV. While watching, he writes something on a piece of paper. Tonight, I manage to place myself in a position where I can see the paper. Every time the minute changes on the clock, he writes it down.

I attempt to strike up a conversation.

"Sh! You need to be quiet." Without taking his eyes off the clock, he points by tilting his head toward it. He announces, "I've got to hear what that man is saying."

I'm horrified to watch the disintegration of my husband's mind, and at the same time, the realization that his loss is my loss overwhelms me. I shake my head and walk away.

Days pass, and he tires of the man in the clock. "The minutes aren't going by fast enough," he says. He wants to disconnect it, but he can't find the receptacle. "Unplug this thing."

I reach behind the chest, unplug the cord, and leave the room.

After an hour or so, I hear, "Hey Faye, come in here." Once I'm in the room, he asks, "Will you set this clock for me?"

I plug it back in and reset it. Within a few minutes, he's upset with the time and asks me to disconnect it again. This continues every evening, and after a week, there's still no end in sight. I refuse to cooperate.

Acy asks, "Why do you act that way? You could unplug that if you wanted to."

"I can't remember where the receptacle is," I say.

This gives him an idea. He follows the cord, yanks it out of the wall, and then reconnects it. Now it sits there, flashing and taunting me. When he leaves the bedroom, I slip the plug from the receptacle. Upon his return, I distract him with another clock that actually talks. He tries it out and rejects it. He says he can't understand what it's saying.

The next night, he notices the electric alarm clock on the nightstand. He loses interest in the digital clock.

He's studying the clock's hands. He begins turning the stem that sets the time. He's turning with such intensity, I ask, "What are you doing?"

"I'm unwinding this clock."

I take a deep breath and try to accept that my reality is no longer his reality. If only there was a way I could reach out, touch him, and draw him back.

His hand slows down. "I'm tired. Will you take over for me?"

Not in this lifetime, I think. "I'm too tired right now."

I'm being drawn into this Alzheimer's journey with him.

The next night, I give him an alarm clock he can actually wind. In the middle of the night, I'm startled from my sleep when the alarm sounds. He's set the alarm by mistake. I hear a commotion somewhere in the house. I turn off the alarm and hurry to the living room. The cats are flying through the house and seeking a place to hide. One jumps through the room divider, and everything on the shelves scatters into the two rooms it divides. I pick up magazines and a laptop in the living room and pictures and whatnots in the kitchen. It takes me an hour to clean up the mess. I return to bed, but I can't sleep. I lie there and wonder where this Alzheimer's journey will lead us.

The next morning, I notice Acy frowning. He chastises me. "You and the cats woke me up last night."

Biting my lip until I taste blood, I tell myself, *He can't help it. It's Alzheimer's.*

He drinks his coffee while he watches TV in the living room. I'm desperate for one day of peace and quiet. I slip into the bedroom. Holding pliers in one hand, I pick the alarm clock up with the other. I notice my heartbeat is in unison with the ticking clock. My hand moves the pliers closer to the clock. I hesitate while I do a slow burn. I watch as my grip on the pliers breaks the key that sets the alarm. Tears flow as I collapse on the bed, and the stress evaporates from my body. At last, the air moves freely through my lungs. Every fiber of my being wants nothing more than to stay here, but I know I must return to the living room.

There he is. He's studying the pendulum clock that hangs on the wall. *Oh no! Not that clock! That's the clock he gave me for our twenty-fifth wedding anniversary.* He turns and focuses on me. "Why can't you find a clock that keeps the right time?"

"I don't know. I guess they don't make them the way they used to."

He heads toward the kitchen for another cup of coffee, and I slip my clock into the closet. I move another clock out of his sight, but I place it where I can see the time.

Next I buy wall clocks. I hang them up over the furniture and out of his reach.

A few weeks later, I pass through the living room and see him with the broom. He taps on the wall clock with the handle.

"What are you doing?"

"I need to fix this clock."

He's not successful because the clock face is covered. I decide there are worse things he could be doing. At least he's safe, and I know where he is.

This continues for several months. Then he finds the perfect timepiece, and his wristwatch becomes his constant companion. I reset it for him several times a day.

Are We Married? Part One

Acy asks to see our marriage certificate. I find this a little odd. He's never shown any interest in it before. I give him a copy, and he studies it closely. "Where did we get married?"

I point to the center of the room. "We were married here, in the living room."

He holds up the certificate. "Can I keep this?"

I put it in a frame, and he hangs it on the wall over the couch.

He tells friends we're married, and they look puzzled, as if wondering why he waited thirty-three years to announce it. He knows who I am, but at times he forgets we're married.

When he's not too busy studying clocks, he studies the marriage certificate. A few weeks into this confusion, he's looking at the marriage certificate on the wall. He asks, "Are we married?"

"Yes," I reply.

Since there is no one close to help care for him, I think he'll be relieved to know he has someone.

This is a big mistake. He denies it. I try to help him understand. This goes on all afternoon. I remind myself, *He can't help it. It's Alzheimer's.*

He lifts the certificate off the wall and holds it out for me to see. For the umpteenth time, he asks, "Are we married?"

I take a deep breath. With a calm voice, I say, "Acy, we were married thirty-three years ago."

His voice is unsteady, "Now, I think the world of you, but I don't want to get married!"

I repeat to myself, *He can't help it. It's Alzheimer's.*

The more I try explaining it to him, the more belligerent he becomes. My head hurts, I'm exhausted, and my mind takes a break. Without my creative juices, the ability to make up lies to keep him happy fails me. I stop talking, but he insists I answer his questions.

Finally, I don't care if it is Alzheimer's. I stare him right in the eye and tell him, "Look, I don't want to be married to you any more than you do me."

"All right, all right. We'll do it your way. We'll get married," he says.

I pray, *Lord, keep me from saying or doing something I'll regret.*

Acy hangs the certificate back on the wall, settles in on the couch, and takes a nap. I sit and seethe. I can't take another day like this. I lift the framed copy from the wall and throw it in the trash.

He wakes from his nap and doesn't mention the marriage certificate until bedtime. We go to bed, and I'm greeted with, "Are we married?"

"Don't worry. We're not married."

"Then what are we going to do about that thing?"

"What thing?"

"That thing on the wall in the living room."

"You don't need to worry about that either. I threw it away."

For once, he doesn't have a comeback. I relax in the peace and quiet. He breaks the silence. "We can still live together and tell people we're married."

"Honey, it's bedtime. Please go to sleep."

"All right, Faye baby. I love you."

"I love you too. Goodnight, sweetheart."

The next day, he's quiet and deep in thought. With some hesitation, I ask, "What's on your mind?"

"I wonder why I don't have any teeth," he answers.

"In 2003 you had oral cancer, and the doctors had to pull them. You can't wear dentures or have dental implants because they removed part of your gums and jawbone during surgery to remove the cancer."

"I don't remember that. You know more about me than I know about myself." He no longer understands why I know personal things about him.

After this, when he questions our relationship, I tell him, "I'm the one who loves you more than anything, and I'll always be here for you."

I quit asking him to remember anything. I resolve to use my new status as a "single person" to my advantage. I no longer seek his approval to do things. This works, because discussing anything with him is difficult. I've learned to expect anything, and if playing along can help make life easier, I go for it.

Our marital status becomes compromised, and things change around here. In his mind, he's not responsible for any of the bills, and worse, he can do anything he wants because he's single and doesn't have to answer to anyone.

That Other Woman
There are three of us in this relationship now. Acy, me, and "that other woman." While I'm using the desktop computer, Acy says, "I'll never learn to use

that computer. I'm giving it to my sister. Why don't you get one of your own?"

I turn off the desktop and open the laptop he gave me for Christmas.

"That doesn't belong to you either."

"Who does it belong to?"

"It belongs to that other woman."

"What other woman?"

"I can't remember her name. I wish I could."

I close the laptop. *He can't help it. It's Alzheimer's.*

"Doesn't anything in this house belong to me?"

"No."

"Not even my clothes?"

"The clothes are yours. That's all."

At this point, he believes anything that is mine belongs to his sister or "that other woman," whose name he can't remember. I don't know what I'll do if he starts giving my possessions away. He also thinks that anything I've given him was given to him by his mother. I feel totally rejected. I know he's sick, but I am too. I'm sick of being treated as a stranger in my own home.

Then I remember, *He can't help it. It's Alzheimer's. I hate Alzheimer's.* I bide my time and hope this will pass.

I need to use my laptop. I lift it from the shelf and sit down in my rocker. I settle in and lift the lid.

"Don't open that. It doesn't belong to you."

"Who does it belong to?"

"That other woman. I can't remember her name. I wish I could."

Acy's always been a control freak. I nicknamed him Hitler. I learned early in our marriage to stand up to him. At least, I could always reason with him. At this point, he doesn't know what he's saying, and his reasoning button is gone. Still, I need that laptop.

I stand up and place the laptop on the desk. My chest tightens, as I rummage through my receipts. *If nothing around here belongs to me, then there's no reason for me to stay.* I dig deeper into the stack. Here's my receipt. This laptop means a lot to me, and Alzheimer's or no Alzheimer's, it's mine.

Acy's sitting by the laptop. My heart races, and my breathing is heavy. I lay the receipt down next to the laptop. I keep my voice low but firm. "Do you see this receipt?"

"Yes."

"Do you see the serial number written on it?"

"Yes."

"Isn't it the same number that's on the laptop?"

He looks at both numbers. "Yes."

I point to my name on the receipt. "This proves the laptop belongs to me."

He studies the receipt and thinks it over. "Well, that other woman must have a laptop like yours."

One of these days, I'm going to beat the crap out of "that other woman!" I know. I know. He can't help it. It's Alzheimer's.

"That other woman" is my constant companion. His sister informs me that Acy called her while I was at the doctor's. She asked him where I was, and he said I left with that other woman.

Today, when I leave and return home, he asks, "Who was that other woman in the car with you?"

"Who did it look like?"

"I don't know. I couldn't see her face."

"I don't know who it was either."

He pauses for a moment. "When are you going to marry me?"

I'm not sure if he's talking to me or "that other woman." "When you find someone to marry us," I say.

"I can't think of anyone right now."

"Let me know when you do."

We could renew our vows, but he can't make up his mind if he wants to be married or not.

Whose Car is it?

We own a car and two trucks. Most of the time, I drive the car, and he drives the trucks. We have always referred to the car as mine and the trucks as his. Recently, he informed me the car isn't mine. I know I should stop saying "my car," but it slips out without me realizing it.

It's race day, and we have settled in to watch the Sprint Cup races. In the excitement of racing, wrecking, and pitting, I mention my car. Acy springs to his feet, crosses his arms, and towers over me. "I'm telling you right now, that car doesn't belong to you!" he snaps. "Where's the registration card?"

I scurry to the car, find the registration card, and head back to the living room. I hand the card to him, and he sees our names on the card. The vein in his forehead throbs, and he explodes in a rage. "I don't care what that card says! It's wrong! It's not mine, and it's not yours! It belongs to that other woman!"

I'm standing too close, so I back away. I make sure I don't turn my back. His breathing quickens, and I glance down as his chest heaves. I look back up, and there it is—his Alzheimer's stare. He stands rigid, with unblinking eyes that glare at me. I stand my ground. *Do not run, and show no fear.* After what seems like forever, he turns and stomps out of the room.

A half hour later, he returns. I'm sitting in my rocker, and he sits down on the footstool in front of me. He takes my hand, and I can see the remorse in his eyes. "I'm sorry I became so angry at you. I can't remember why I was upset, but I was wrong to get that angry."

I'm speechless. In all the time we've been married, he's never apologized.

Tears slide down my face. "It's all right, baby. I know you couldn't help it. I just need a car to go to the store and the doctor. You'll let me use your truck for that, won't you?"

"Why sure."

I try to humor him. "If that woman comes back, she can have the car."

"No, she's not getting the car back," he replies.

The tension is gone, and I tease him. "Since I don't have a car, don't you think you ought to buy me one?"

"That's all right. You can have that one."

He thinks he's outwitted me. We laugh, and for a while, things are back to normal. Once more, the car belongs to me.

Deeds

"Hey Faye, come here a minute."

I'm being summoned to the bedroom. I stick my head in the door. "What do you want?"

"These deeds aren't right. I need to see a lawyer. Do you know one?"

I see copies of our deeds spread across the bed. "I can't think of one right now."

I leave the room and wonder where this will lead.

He turns to his friends for help. When they inform me, I ask them not to help him.

He wants me to go to the courthouse.

"I want you to get copies of the tax tickets."

"I can't climb the hill to the courthouse."

"I can't either," he says.

He's determined, and after a few weeks of non-stop badgering, he demands, "Take me to see a lawyer! I need to get these deeds fixed!"

"What's wrong with the deeds?"

"I need to take your name off them. I don't know why Dad put your name on the deeds. He promised this land to me."

He can't help it. It's Alzheimer's.

He picks up the phone book and searches through it.

"What are you doing?"

"I'm looking for a lawyer."

I sit down beside him and watch as he scans the white pages. "Can I help?"

He hands me the book. "Here. You look awhile."

After turning a few pages, I tell him, "I'm not having any luck either."

He becomes frustrated, grabs the book, and pitches it across the table. I wait until he takes a nap, then I go through the phone books and black out all the lawyers' names.

One lawyer advertises once a week in the local paper. If he sees this ad, it will only bring more confusion.

Today's the day the lawyer's ad appears in the paper. When it's time for the paper delivery, I entice

Acy into the bedroom with a promise to do whatever his heart desires. Afterward, while he is in the bathroom, I dash to the paper box. With a Magic Marker in hand, I retrieve the paper and black out the ad. I return to find Acy sitting on the couch. I hand him the paper. "Here's your paper."

He gives me a kiss to show his gratitude. "Thank you, Dottie Faye."

"You're welcome, sweetie."

This will be my MO until his deed obsession is over. It feels as if I have resorted to the world's oldest profession. My price? My sanity.

When I get the opportunity, I confiscate his copies of the deeds and put them under lock and key. The next day, he misses them.

"Have you seen my deeds?"

"Can't say that I have."

"Well, I can't find them."

"They'll turn up somewhere."

He searches for them, and in the meantime, I gather up all the deeds and tax tickets and put them in a safe at the bank. He frets for a time, then moves on to other things.

Is it Hot in Here?
Acy fixates on the air conditioner. "Don't turn that thing on. It bothers my sinuses."

"Why don't you watch TV in the bedroom? I ask. I'll cool down the kitchen and living room. Then you can come back."

"I'm not going to the bedroom, so you leave it off."

It's been days, and the heat in the house is unbearable. I manage to turn the air conditioner on when he sleeps. I buy a personal size fan, and hide it under the table beside my rocker. He sits on the other side of the room.

"Don't turn that on either!" he yells. "It bothers me too."

I take the fan and stay in the bedroom. This is where he finds me.

"It's not fair. I don't have a fan. You need to go back to the living room."

I move to the living room, and he makes me turn off the fan. I retreat back to the bedroom.

The temperature reaches ninety degrees in the kitchen. I try using the fan, but it does little more than blow the hot air around the room.

"It's too hot in here to cook," I say. "I'm not going to risk passing out from the heat. If you want your meals, you can go to the bedroom and rest or watch TV, while I cool off the kitchen."

He leaves in a huff and sulks in the bedroom. After this, he goes to the bedroom before meals so

I can cool the house down. This is our new normal the rest of the season.

Bank Account Number One

July finds us dealing with the bank accounts. Our accounts are joint accounts, but I'm the one who handles our finances. He's never written a check, nor has he ever looked at a bank statement, until now. He finds a bank statement and can't understand it.

He wants me to explain it to him. He seems satisfied with my explanation, but soon after, I hear him talking on the phone in the bedroom. He's talking to his niece who works at the bank. He asks her to bring him some checks. After he hangs up, I go to the other end of the house and call back. I tell his niece we have plenty of checks.

When she doesn't bring him any checks, he turns to me. "Will you go to the bank and get me some checks?"

"What do you need checks for?"

"I don't have any."

"You don't write checks."

"Will you close the account, and bring me my money?"

"The account doesn't have much money in it."

"I don't care. I want my money."

I remind him, "This account was opened for me. We decided I should have a checking account with a small amount of cash, so I could carry the checkbook when I go out. I carry it in case I have an emergency and need money. If I close it and something happens, I won't have the money to return home."

"Oh. Well then, I'll put some more money in it."

"That's all right. I have enough."

He never mentions this account again.

Bank Account Number Two

Acy is obsessed with his money.

"I want you to fix my checks so they come to the mailbox," he says.

"I'm not sure I can do that."

"Well then, you go to the bank and get my money."

"Now, Acy, in all the years we've been together we've never argued over money, and I don't intend to start now."

He drops the subject for a few days. One night, he goes to bed at seven o'clock. An hour later, he yells, "Hey Faye, come in here." He sees me in the doorway and says, "I got a call from the bank. They told me people are taking my money."

"Are you sure they called?"

"Yes. I need to get my money. They say someone is taking it."

"That would be me. I'm the only one with access to the account."

"No, no. Not you. You would never do that. It's someone working at the bank."

"Honey, the bank's closed. Why don't you lie back and watch some TV?"

"OK, but this needs to be taken care of tomorrow."

Morning comes, and we make it through the day without mention of the bank. He retires to the bedroom around six o'clock. I sit down at the computer. Things are quiet until about half past seven.

I hear a thump, and the bedroom door swings open. Acy steps out and marches down the hall. He stops in front of me. His unblinking eyes glare down at me, and his jaw muscles are twitching. I recognize his Alzheimer's stare. A feeling of déjà vu washes over me. I stand up, push my chair back, and brace myself for what's to come.

"I'm going to the bank and get my money."

"Why do you want to do that?"

"Because someone's stealing it."

"We can't do anything about it right now. We have to wait for the bank to open. How about you and I work this out tomorrow?"

While he thinks this over, his jaw relaxes, and the light appears in his eyes. He saunters back to the bedroom.

To stop this confrontation every evening, I find places to hide. I go for long walks or hide on the neighbors' back porches.

I don't get away quick enough tonight. He calls me to the bedroom, and demands money. "Go to the bank and get me a thousand dollars."

"Which bank?"

"I can't remember the name."

"Is it time for your doctor's appointment?" I've been told to try to distract him.

"What's that have to do with going to the bank? Go get my money, or I'll get it myself!"

My distraction skills need a lot of work. "Why do you want a thousand dollars?" I ask.

"I need to buy something."

"What do you need to buy?"

"I'm single. I don't have to tell you."

"If you don't want to tell me, I'll go back to the living room."

Five minutes later he follows. "I don't need anything. I just want the money."

"The bank is closed now. It'll be open tomorrow."

This time he doesn't forget. The next morning, his first words are, "You don't have to get me a thousand. Just get me five hundred."

"First, you need to shave."

This distraction works. While he's shaving, he calls to me. "Faye baby, come here a minute."

I enter the bathroom. "What do you want?"

He looks at me with sad eyes and an unsure smile. With a tender voice, he asks, "Won't you ever kiss me again?"

Alzheimer's keeps him from knowing we are married, but he hasn't forgotten my kiss. I realize Alzheimer's can't destroy the love in his heart.

I cross the room and pull him close to me. With our bodies entwined, I give him a tight squeeze, kiss him, and tell him, "I'll always love you."

His arms tighten around me. It's as if he's afraid to let go. "I love you too."

I suspect what he really wants to know is if things will ever be normal again. He's forgotten about the money.

He decides to nap, and I turn on the computer to head for TheAlzheimerSpouse.com. I discuss the money problem with the group, and we agree that Acy must be sundowning. He goes to bed early, and with nothing else to do, he starts worrying about his money. I start going with him. After he falls asleep, I move back to the living room. This seems to ease the sundowning, and he appears to have forgotten about the bank.

Days pass without Acy mentioning the bank. It's evening, and I'm paying bills. After some time sleeping in the bedroom, Acy awakens and decides he wants a glass of water. He sees me sitting at the kitchen table. He moves toward the table, and watches me write checks for the bills.

Self-pity fills his voice. "I don't have any money in the bank to pay bills."

I feel sorry for him. Not wanting him to worry, I say, "You have money in the bank to pay bills."

He changes faster than Dr. Jekyll to Mr. Hyde. "I don't have any bills! You go get me my money!"

I'm so tired. I don't try to explain, so he rants and raves while I continue to pay bills. I vow never to mention the word "bank" again. Late at night, when he sleeps, I write the checks for the bills.

He resumes his crusade for money. I decide to appease him. I bring him money from the bank. I only do this when he asks. The problem accelerates when he starts wanting money every day.

One day, he informs me, "Dorothy's not doing her job."

"What do you mean?"

"She didn't give me my money."

"Give her a little time. She hasn't gone to the bank yet," I say.

He goes to the bedroom and spreads his money on the bed. I follow him. I want to know if he can count. He keeps glancing at me. It appears he's trying to decide if he can trust me. After a few minutes of struggling to count his money, he asks me to count it for him.

At that point, I remove money from his stash and give him the same money each day. I learn to lie, lie, and lie some more. This doesn't always work, but it cuts down on the trips to the bank.

Friends tell me that Acy has asked them to drive him to the bank, promising to make it worth their time. I worry he'll find someone to drive him to the bank and help him empty our accounts, while I still have checks coming in. I don't want to be charged with writing bad checks, so I take precautions. I'm forced to draw some of the funds from our accounts and put them in a new one in my name only. I sign for the bank to hold my statements, and I pick them up there.

I don't want to do this. Every fiber of my being tells me this is wrong. I'm taking his life from him one step at a time. I think, *I can't help it. It's Alzheimer's.*

When I return home, he's sitting on the couch. "Where have you been?"

"Out running some errands."

He announces, "I'm so lucky I have someone I can trust."

Guilt consumes me. I hang my head. I'm reminded of the many times we've talked about how lucky we are to have each other. We've always known if something happened to one of us, the other could be trusted to handle everything. I realize he's trying to tell me he knows that time has come.

It occurs to me that not only is Alzheimer's causing him to do things he wouldn't normally do, but it's also forcing me to do things I don't want to do. *I hate Alzheimer's!*

CHAPTER 4

2008: PART TWO

Whose House is This?

There's a new slant on things. I've managed to reclaim my belongings. Acy no longer has any idea who they belong to. He doesn't know the house belongs to us. He thinks it belongs to someone else.

"Faye, will you help me fix up the old house?"

"Why do you want to do that?"

"Someone is going to throw me out of here."

"No one can throw you out. You and I own this house."

"I don't think so. I'd better find some place to live."

"Don't worry. I won't let anyone evict you."

"I'm not sure about that."

No way am I going to show him the deed. Instead, I write a note on a piece of paper that states he will always have a home here, and I hand it to him.

"Would you mind signing this for me?"

I sign the note, and he puts it in his nightstand drawer. From time to time, he takes it out and looks at it.

The nightstand drawer becomes a permanent home for the note.

Delusions: Part One

Acy's become obsessed with taking off all his clothes when he has a bowel movement. He pulls them off, folds them, and leaves them outside the bathroom door. He believes they will get dirty in the bathroom. After a time, this mushrooms into a delusion of him being constipated. I notice he's taking too many stool softeners. I try to limit him. He refuses to listen, so I hide the pills.

I'm making the bed this morning, and Acy yells from the kitchen, "Hey Faye, I need some stool softeners."

I hasten to the kitchen to find him searching the cabinets.

"We don't have any," I tell him.

"Well, go the store and buy me some."

"The store doesn't have any either."

"There has to be a store somewhere that sells stool softeners."

"I'll be sure to watch for them."

His Afrin episode in 2007 crosses my mind, and I worry he may go in search of laxatives.

I need to spread the word to the business establishments he frequents. I realize this is only a temporary solution until his appointment with Dr. Trent in a few days. My first stop is the pharmacy. I explain the situation and leave my phone number. The pharmacist says she's known for a while something is wrong with Acy. She tells the cashier at the counter not to sell Acy any laxatives.

At my next stop, I enter the store and approach the cashier. He's Acy's friend and has known about Acy's illness for some time. He's told me he wants to help in any way he can. I reach the counter, and he asks about Acy. I explain the situation and ask that he not sell Acy any laxatives. Before I have time to offer my phone number, he turns on me. "I saw Acy yesterday, and there wasn't anything wrong with him. If he comes in here and wants to buy laxatives, I'll sell them to him."

As I turn and leave, I think, *With friends like that, who needs enemas?*

I continue on my mission, and everyone else is willing to help. I make note of the store that isn't safe for Acy to patronize. As I travel down the Alzheimer's journey, it doesn't take long to learn who our true friends are.

During his appointment with Dr. Trent, he tells her he's constipated and needs something for relief. I motion to her this isn't true. She tells him laxatives have been taken off the market.

We leave, and when we arrive home, he's still distressed. I have no luck relieving his anxiety. Even though it's time for Dr. Trent's office to close, I go back and talk to her. "Acy's obsessed with his bowel movements, and I can't reason with him," I inform her.

"I'm more worried about you," she says. "When we started talking about laxatives, I could see fear in your face."

"I fight with him constantly to keep him from taking too much medicine," I say. "I'm afraid someone, not aware of the situation, will help him overdose."

She focuses on me instead of Acy's problem. "You're a prisoner in your own home. You need to get him out of there."

"I don't want to do that. After all, it's his home too."

"He shouldn't be in the house. He could hurt you."

She has no idea that I'm already hurt to the core.

"Are there any guns in the house?" she asks.

"Yes."

She shakes her head. "You need to get those out of the house."

"I know," I reply. I also know they should be removed safely.

"Does he have money?"

"Yes."

"You should confiscate all the money."

I draw the line. "Before he quit smoking, I promised any money he saved would be his to keep. I'll not go back on my word. Besides, any money he has belongs to him."

"At least consider getting him out of the house."

"He does qualify for a nursing home through the VA," I say. "I've tried to persuade him to see a psychiatrist at the VA hospital, but he refuses. He knows that's the first step to being declared incompetent."

"You need to check into this."

"I'm working on it."

She calls the pharmacy and writes a prescription. "Take this to the pharmacy. Let's see if we can humor him until this delusion passes. Be aware, there will be another one to deal with when this one subsides. He will go from one thing to another."

I leave the office and go to the pharmacy. The pharmacist fills the prescription. I return home and give Acy the bottle of pills I bought at the pharmacy. It's a prescription bottle with "laxatives" written on the front. Inside are Tic Tacs. He puts one in his mouth, removes it, and asks, "Am I supposed to swallow this with water, or eat it?"

"You can take it either way."

After taking a few Tic Tacs, he tells me, "These pills aren't working. You need to go back to the doctor and tell her I need something stronger."

"This type of pill takes a few days to work."

Two days pass, and his mood mellows. He decides the "laxatives" I gave him help.

I drive to the store, and when I return home, I discover Acy has a visitor. I pull in the garage and see our neighbor, Jim, descending the steps. I park and step out of the car. I notice his 6'2" frame shudders as he crosses the concrete.

I move toward him, and hear the strain in his voice as he says, "There's something wrong with Acy. He says his bowels haven't moved in a week, and he wants to know where to get ex-lax. I told him the store down the road sold it, and there may be some at my house. He wants me to give him some before his intestines explode. I don't know what to do."

Jim finds himself in the middle of our nightmare. I prepare myself to deal with two distraught men. "I'll carry the groceries in and then tend to Acy," I tell Jim.

Jim helps with the groceries, and I enter the living room. Acy is pacing back and forth. Beads of sweat cover his face. He shouts, "Dorothy, I want you to go to the store and get me some ex-lax!"

"I've checked at the store, and there isn't any." I'm afraid if he gets his hands on a box, he'll take all the pills at one time.

"Then go to Jim and Bessie's."

"I'll call her to see if they have any left." I don't want to leave these two alone. I call from the bedroom so my voice will be muffled. "Bessie, do you have any ex-lax?"

"Yes."

"No," I say in a low voice, then louder, "You don't have any?"

"All right," she says, playing along.

I'll explain it to her later. I return to the living room. "Bessie used the last one she had."

Acy pulls me to the bathroom and points to the toilet. "See? My bowels haven't moved all day."

I don't have to look. The odor drifts from the bowl. Staring at the proof in the bowl, he still believes his bowels haven't moved. He refuses to flush the toilet, and he won't let me.

We move back to the living room, and he asks Jim, "Will you give me some ex-lax?"

Jim's voice breaks, as he says, "I can't give you any. Dorothy won't let me."

Acy now knows I'm the reason he doesn't have any ex-lax. He turns on me and raves, "Why won't you let me have any? If my bowels don't move soon, my guts will burst, and I'll get my clothes dirty. It will be your fault. Why do you treat me this way?"

"If your guts burst, you'll have more to worry about than dirty clothes," I say. I recall a notebook he's been using to keep a record of his bowel movements. I search the coffee table. I find his notebook and show it to him. I point at today's entry. "See? You wrote down what time your bowels moved."

"I didn't write that! You're trying to trick me! If you don't get me some ex-lax, I'll get the gun and blow out my brains!" He drifts toward the hall.

I'm afraid for him. With his dementia, it's possible he may try. He has five loaded firearms in the house. People could get hurt—or worse—if they try to stop him.

Jim tells me, "You need to get the guns out of the house."

"They're in the bedroom. Do you want to remove them?" I ask.

Jim replies, "No way!"

"OK. When I can find a safe way, I'll handle it."

I need a diversion. I pick the phone up, call Alan, and ask him to talk with Acy. I hand Acy the phone, and say, "Alan wants to talk with you."

The distraction works. While they talk, Jim eases out the door and heads for his house. Acy and Alan have a sensible conversation, and Acy's back to his old self. When they are through talking, he hands me the phone.

Alan tells me, "I couldn't tell there's anything wrong with him."

The next day, I pay a visit to Jim and Bessie. I explain what's been transpiring and how long it's been going on. Jim keeps repeating, "But he's the smartest man I know."

I think, *He's not stupid. He has Alzheimer's.* Since Acy only goes out in public on his lucid days, Jim, Bessie, and many others find it hard to believe he has a problem. They can't deny it any longer.

I return home to find Acy walking the floor. "Why won't you buy me some laxatives?"

"I can't find any."

"You could if you wanted to. Why are you so mean to me? I wouldn't treat you this way."

"I'm doing all I can to help you."

He grows weary and takes a nap on the couch.

I use the phone in the bedroom and call the Alzheimer's Association's hotline. A nice lady answers, and I tell her about my situation. I say that I'm out of ideas to humor him. Try as she might, she can't come up with any new ideas.

I turn on my computer and head for TheAlzheimerSpouse.com. On the message board, I state my predicament. By bedtime, I have a list of ideas to choose from. I study the list and pick one.

Daylight finds me sitting in my car. I'm in the parking lot at Walmart. I put the idea I have chosen into action. I buy a bag of M&M's and two boxes of ex-lax. I return to the car and remove the blue ex-lax pills from the boxes. I replace them with the blue M&M's. As I leave Walmart, I prepare myself for what awaits me at home. I arrive home, and he's waiting in the living room.

"Did you find me any ex-lax?"

"I sure did." Feeling generous, I present him with both boxes.

He opens a box and looks at the M&Ms. "Why is there an *m* on each one?"

"The *m* stands for 'maximum.'"

He takes the boxes and sets them on a shelf over the kitchen sink.

Days later, we're in the kitchen, and he points to the ex-lax boxes and says, "I didn't take any of those. I'm afraid to."

I give him a hug and try to reassure him. "Well, we'll keep them here in case you need them again. OK, sweetie?"

"OK."

He no longer talks about being constipated. I think about all the stress he has put me and others through in the past weeks. *He can't help it. It's Alzheimer's.*

Guns and Trucks

The gun issue is a serious problem. Acy was an expert marksman in the army. He loves to hunt. He told me once he wouldn't stay in a house without his guns.

I'm aware that if I make my move too soon and his dementia hasn't progressed far enough, he can and will fight back. I can't remove the guns from the house until I disable the trucks. As long as he's able to drive, he can acquire and hide a gun. I would rather deal with the ones I know about than be surprised by one later on. I decide to remove the bullets from the guns for now. He has two pistols plus a revolver in his nightstand drawer. A shotgun stands by the bed within arm's reach, and the rifle is in the next bedroom. All are loaded, and I know nothing about unloading them. I do a search on the Internet. I wait for Acy to drive down the road to put gas in the car, and I make my move.

I start with the small pistol and remove the magazine, but I don't know how to get the bullet from the chamber. I pray, *Lord, I can't do this by myself. I need someone to show me what to do.* I take the gun out the back door. Other than the BB pistol, I've never fired a gun, and I hesitate now. I figure the safest way is to aim for the sky. I make sure nothing is in the path of fire and no birds are close by. I fire the gun, and walk back into the house. I try to figure out how to remove the magazine from the large pistol. I hear a knock at the front door. I open it, and there stands Alan. God heard and answered my prayer. He says,

"I thought I'd stop by to see how you and Acy are doing."

I show him the pistol. "Do you know how to unload this?"

"Yes," he says.

I panic and change my mind. "We'd better not do this. It's too dangerous. Acy could return home any minute."

"I'm not leaving here until I empty that pistol," he says.

"OK. You go behind the house to unload the pistol. I'll stay in the front and watch for Acy."

Alan empties the pistol and leaves.

That night, as Acy sleeps, I go to the other room and remove the magazine from the rifle. I wait to empty the revolver and shotgun because I feel there is a good chance he will notice the bullets missing. I buy some childproof locks. Instructions say not to use them on loaded guns.

Weeks later, Acy mentions that the owner of the service station pumped his gas for him. I make a trip to the service station to talk to the owners. They tell me Acy forgot how to use the pumps. The thought enters my mind, *Even though he can still drive, he might forget which one is the brake and which one is the gas.* This is my cue. I've never put gas in the car, so they show me how to use the pumps. Acy has mentioned showing me how the pumps work but never got around to it.

When I return home, he's ready to take the car and fill it up. I tell him I've been pumping my own gas, ever since he showed me how. He hesitates, and I see a puzzled look on his face. I can tell he isn't sure if he showed me or not. He accepts that he has, and he doesn't make an issue of me taking over this chore.

It's time to "lose" his keys. I start with my car first and hide his key. He searches for a short time and quits. He doesn't drive the car much, but he knows I have a key. "Let me borrow your key."

"You can't borrow my key."

"Why?"

"If you lose it, I won't be able to use the car."

He accepts this without an argument. One down. Two to go.

He keeps losing the keys to the trucks, so my job is made easier. "Hey Faye, can you help me find my keys?"

I find them in his coat pocket. He loses the keys again, and we search but can't locate them. When I find them, I put them in a locked jewelry chest. As he hunts for them, I call all his mechanic friends and explain to them about Acy's problem. I ask them not to assist him if he contacts them. He calls friends, but they can't help.

He tries to find a way to start the trucks, and I adjust to the idea that I no longer have someone to come to my aid if I have car trouble. Every time I go out, I cry because I'm reminded he can no longer drive. I feel more guilt from this than anything else I've done. I must not lose sight of why this is necessary. I know where to lay the blame. *I can't help it. It's Alzheimer's!*

I ask Alan to stop by and put the trucks up on blocks. I tell Acy that will keep the tires from flattening on the ground. This is true, but I also hope it will stop him from thinking about driving them.

Now that he no longer has a vehicle to drive, it's time to remove the guns. While he eats in the kitchen, I'm in the bedroom. I lock the bedroom door and remove the bullets from the revolver. I can't figure out how to unload the shotgun. I can see the potential for danger. It's important to have a strategy. I decide to remove them from the bedroom. Once I move the guns out of his reach, I will find a way to remove them from the house. If I'm caught, I'll have to deal with an angry, demented man, who has a loaded shotgun and can't reason.

I realize someone needs to know what's happening in my home. I call Alan and tell him what I'm about to do. He says his brother, Jack, a deputy, is on duty. He gives me the number where I can reach Jack. Jack is Acy's friend, and I'm comfortable confiding in him. I call Jack and tell him what I'm planning to do. Acy hasn't been declared incompetent and hasn't broken any laws, so Jack isn't allowed to intervene. He wants me to keep him informed of how things transpire. One thing I know for sure—I'm not waiting, until Acy shoots me or someone else, to seek help. Jack says to go ahead and put the childproof lock on the loaded shotgun. I tell him I'll stay in touch.

It's evening, and Acy's in the bedroom. He's watching TV. I lie down beside him. He goes to the bathroom when a commercial comes on. It's time to move. I'm out of my league here. *Lord, guide my hands, and do your stuff.*

I remove the pocket-sized pistol from the back of the drawer, proceed to the next bedroom, lock the door behind me, and secure the pistol in a small fireproof safe. I go back to the bedroom and wait. When he goes to the bathroom again, I take the large pistol from the drawer and put it with the small one. I wait to move the revolver and shotgun. He sometimes takes a quick peek at the revolver before he goes to sleep, and his shotgun stands by the bed. I'm afraid he'll miss them before I have a chance to hide them properly.

Acy turns out the light and falls asleep. I lie in bed and listen to the sound of his breathing to make sure he's in a deep sleep. I crawl around the bed to his nightstand. I ease the drawer open and slip out the revolver. I close the drawer and decide I don't want to go through this again. Being careful not to break the silence, I stand up, grab the shotgun, and dash through the darkness to the security of the bedroom across the hall. I lock the door behind me, and place the revolver with the pistols. The shotgun is too long to hide here. I make sure the hall's clear and take it to a third bedroom. I lock the door. I attach a gun lock to the shotgun, pull the dresser out, and hide the gun under the dresser. I'm not finished.

I still need to hide the rifle. Since it's not in the room where he sleeps, I think this will be easier. I fetch the rifle, insert a gun lock on it, and hide it alongside the shotgun. As I push the dresser back in place, I breathe a sigh of relief.

I open the door to leave, and there he stands. We're face-to-face, and I'm frozen to the floor. He asks, "Now, what's this all about?"

I struggle to find my voice. I say the first thing that comes to my mind. "I can't find my cat. I thought she might be in here."

He accepts this and heads to the bathroom. I know this is a short-term fix. At least now he doesn't have a loaded gun at arm's length.

The next day, he takes his nap, and I disappear into the room where the pistols and revolver are stored. I remove them from the safe and install gun locks on them. I lay them back in the safe and lock it in the file cabinet.

A week later, Acy discovers his shotgun's missing. He tries to remember who he loaned it to. He doesn't know what to do, but I know what I have to do. It's time to execute the last part of my plan.

The neighbors have agreed to keep the guns if I can get them out of the house. A few nights pass before I get the opportunity to move the rifle. Acy's in our bedroom watching TV. I slip into the other bedroom to fetch the rifle. I ease the door open to make sure the hall is clear. I clutch the rifle close to me. I flee down the hall on wings of faith, through the living room, across the foyer, and out the door. I start across the road toward the neighbors' house. If he looks out the living room window, he can see their front porch. I hold the rifle in front of me with my back to our house. I hasten to the back porch and leave it there. When I return home, I call the neighbors and tell them where to find it.

Acy is home day and night, and the loaded shotgun worries me. I know a mistake could have serious consequences. He's reclining on the couch and watching TV. His back is to the hall. I decide it's time to make my move. I go down the hall and into the bedroom. I retrieve the gun from under the dresser and wrap it in a blanket. My only protection is the gun lock. I check and make sure his back is still turned. I carry the gun through the hall. As I pass him, the back of his head is about two feet away from the loaded shotgun. He doesn't turn around, and I hurry to the garage and place the gun in my car's trunk. I don't want to take the chance of Acy seeing me cross the road with his loaded shotgun. I have my phone with me, and I call Alan. He agrees to meet me at the Dollar Store. I make my excuses to Acy and drive to the store, where I hand the shotgun over to Alan. He unloads it and transfers it to his truck. Since the handguns are secured inside the filing cabinet, I don't feel the urgency to remove them.

The day after Thanksgiving, I return home from shopping to find a hostile husband. He meets me at the door. It seems he waited for my departure to look for the rifle. "What have you done with my rifle?"

"What are you talking about?"

"You go back down the road and get my rifle!"

He's not aware I moved it weeks ago and it's across the road.

I'm standing there, trying to decide if I should leave in the car or go next door. He slams the door, and I hear the lock click. *Good. I didn't want to go in there anyway.* I decide not to involve Jim in this. It's better if Acy doesn't know who my accomplice is.

A short time passes, and the door opens. He steps away from the door. I'm not sure if he has cooled down or if I'm being lured into the house. I know I'll have to face him sometime. I cautiously climb the steps leading toward the door. I have an inkling of what a condemned person must feel during that last walk. I move slowly through the foyer and into the living room to sit and wait.

Acy sits on the couch across from me. "Dorothy, why won't you go get my rifle? Why would you take it? Someone else had to help you. You wouldn't do this by yourself. Why would you let someone talk you into this?"

I have no answers for him.

After a thought, he says, "Did you do this because you're afraid of me?"

I lower my head. His mood seems to change. He appears tranquil. With a gentle voice, he asks, "Who helped you do this?" I sit quietly, and anger rises in his voice. "Someone had to help you with this. When I find out who, I'm going to kill them!"

There's no way I'll tell him. He threatens me, "If you don't return my rifle, I'll take a warrant out for you and have you put in jail."

Could it be any worse than this? I respond, "All right, but know that if I'm in jail, they won't let me out every day to cook your meals for you."

He thinks this over and drops the interrogation for now. It's time for him to eat and he's hungry.

I keep Jack updated on the situation. He advises me to call him if Acy wants to file a report. If Acy contacts the state police, Jack says, I should tell them Acy has Alzheimer's and for them to contact him so he can explain the circumstances. He also tells me, if I have a problem with Acy, I should call him at home, instead of 911. Jack worries that the police may send someone who doesn't understand, and may not know how to handle the situation.

I continue with my strategy to remove the guns. While he's in the bedroom watching TV, I remove the handguns, along with the safe, from the filing cabinet. His guns are his personal property, and I don't have his permission to remove them from the house. I write and sign a note for Jim and Bessie that states why they have his guns. I place the note in the safe along with the guns, and deliver them next door. I keep the key.

Acy discovers his handguns are missing and vows to buy another gun. He has gun buddies who will sell or loan him one, and he still knows how to use the phone. I contact his friends that I think may loan or sell him a gun, and they help spread the word.

I decide to rid the house of the ammunition. Since Christmas is close at hand, I put the ammunition in a shoebox and wrap it in Christmas wrapping paper. While Acy sits at the table and eats, I step up my pace and move toward the door. When I pass by him, he asks, "What's that you're carrying?"

"I'm going next door to take a Christmas gift to Bessie and Jim."

He accepts this explanation, and continues eating.

When I arrive at the neighbors' house, I tell them not to get excited. It's not a Christmas gift. Jim opens the package and puts the ammunition with the guns. I return home, and Acy's watching TV. He tires and goes to bed without another thought of the "Christmas gift."

Acy hasn't mentioned the guns for some time. Today, while looking out the window at Jim and Bessie's house, he informs me that he knows where his guns are, and he knows they are close by. As usual, I don't say anything. He seems satisfied with this and quits asking about them.

I hope I never, never, ever have to take a man's guns from him. It's the hardest thing I have ever done. It's a hell of its own. Have I stopped loving Acy? Not for a minute. I've lived with him and his guns for thirty-three years, and I know this is totally out of character for him. *He can't help it. It's Alzheimer's.*

Christmas Cards

Christmas is a distraction from the guns and driving. Acy loves the Christmas tree, and together we decorate it and the house. Afterward, he arranges the gifts under the tree, and I start putting the unused decorations back in the closet.

I hear, "Hey Faye."

I step into the living room, and Acy's observing our work. "What's your problem?" I ask.

"There aren't enough presents under the tree. You need to buy some more."

"All right, sweetie. I'll start shopping tomorrow."

There is no sign of his illness, and it feels like a traditional holiday. Then the first Christmas cards arrive, and he becomes confused. He's upset with the way the cards from his family are addressed to us. "Why would they put your name on my cards?"

"Because I live here too."

"Well, your name's not Steele. They've made a mistake."

He can't help it. It's Alzheimer's.

He finishes opening the cards and asks, "Will you buy me some cards to send? You should get some for yourself too."

I can see it now. Everyone will wonder why they are receiving a card from him and another from me. "I've already bought cards and put them in the mail," I tell him.

I keep Christmas low-key. Friends and family visit before Christmas. On Christmas Day, it's just the two of us. We have a traditional celebration with turkey and the trimmings. Acy always hands out our gifts. He picks up the first gift, and his shoulders droop. He stares at it. He turns to me, and with a chin that trembles and eyes that plead, he asks, "Can you read this for me?"

I read the name, and he shows me another one. "I can't make these names out."

I tell him the name on the gift. I try to hide my tears as I help him with the rest.

CHAPTER 5
2009: PART ONE

Driver's License

Christmas and New Year's Day are behind us, and I'm still dealing with the driving issue. Driving means everything to Acy. He loves to tell of the time he passed his driver's license test. He acquired his permit on his sixteenth birthday. He passed the road test and received his license the next day. I fear confiscating his license will prove a formidable challenge.

I have an appointment with Dr. Trent. During my visit, I ask her, "Would you write me a note to send to the DMV so Acy's license can be suspended?" She hesitates, and I tell her, "He should lose his license while he still knows he needs one."

She nods her head in agreement and writes the note. I send it to the main DMV office.

A few weeks later, Acy receives a letter from the DMV. His license has been suspended. The letter states, that to reinstate his license, he is required to come to their main office. He's slow to understand that this letter means no more driving.

"Honey, you can't drive without your license."

"You're a good driver. You can chauffeur me around."

I know this is too easy.

It's a warm day in January, and I can't pass up the opportunity to wash the car. I return to find Acy in the living room. He watches me enter the room, and says, "Don't fix me much for supper."

"Why not?"

"I'm too upset."

"What's wrong?"

"That letter from the DMV. And I don't even have a gun."

"What does that have to do with the DMV?"

"I'd put a hole in them."

This confirms what I suspected all along. The guns and driving had to be dealt with at the same time. I don't think this is the end of the driving issue.

A new day dawns, and he's still upset. "I didn't do anything wrong. Will you sell me your car?"

"I can't. I need it to go shopping."

"Will you drive me to the DMV?"

"I don't know how to get there."

He looks forlorn. "I don't either."

He sees the governor's name on the notice and snaps, "I'll kill him!"

I know this isn't possible because Acy is not capable of locating him.

Acy loses interest in the letter, and I put it in the safe. I drive him where he wants to go, and he accepts the situation.

He's right. He didn't do anything wrong. He feels he's being punished, and he can't understand why. I hate myself. How can I manipulate Acy's life this way, and still profess to love him more than anything? I remind myself, *It's because I love him that I do this. I can't help it. It's Alzheimer's.*

Valentine's Day

It's Valentine's Day, and Acy loves giving cards and candy. This year is no different.

As I leave home to run errands, he asks, "Will you pick me up a valentine card and a box of candy?"

"Sure. What kind do you want?"

"Pick out one you like."

Of course I buy the prettiest one I can find along with a box of candy. I also find a manly one to give him. Neither card mentions husband or wife. I don't want to go down that road again.

I return home and give him the card. His tradition has always been to retreat to the bedroom and write me a note in the card. This time, he stays there longer than usual, and I'm uneasy.

He appears from the bedroom. He's all smiles, and struts down the hall. He hands me the card and candy. "Here, Faye baby, I bought you something for Valentine's Day."

"Thanks, sweetie," I say. "You sure are good to me."

He beam's as I hand him the one from me. He motions for me to move closer to him. He pulls me under his arm and leans down so we are face-to-face. I give him a light kiss and pull back. He says, "That wasn't much of a kiss." He pulls me close to him, runs his finger down the side of my face, and lifts my chin. My heart races when I feel his warm, moist lips on mine. He takes me back to a time when everything was right with the world.

As quickly as the moment came, it's gone. I am brought back to reality when I open my eyes and see the card. I feel a catch in my throat, and ache for him. Realizing how much he must have struggled signing the card, I read what he's written, 1 2 3 4 5 6 7 8 9.

Through my tears, I smile and say, "This is beautiful. You did a great job with the card this year. Let's set it here on my table, so I can enjoy it."

I think, *At least he can still count.*

When Valentine's Day is over, I put the card in a drawer with the other cards he's given me through the years. I know this will be the last one.

Fire! Fire!

The cold is creeping through the walls this morning. Acy is in a good mood. I decide to warm the bathroom for his bath. I have a new space heater. It uses the latest technology. It won't get hot and can be hung on the wall. The wall I hang it on is made of Sheetrock. I turn the space heater on and go to the living room to sit with Acy. I hear a zapping noise from the heater and go to the bathroom to check on it. I can't see anything wrong, but I turn the heater off to be on the safe side.

I return to the living room and my hand sewing. The fire alarm goes off, and I look up to see a bright light in the bathroom. I scream, "Fire! Fire!"

I race to the bathroom to see fire flicker from inside the heater. Acy is at the door now, and wants me to move out of his way so he can figure out what to do next.

From my experience of the last four years, I know I can no longer rely on him to think fast. I must somehow take control and do what has to be done. I grab the heater by the cord, as I slip it off the wall. Carrying it by the cord, I race through the bathroom and down the hall. When I reach the living room, Acy is there, and he's yelling, "You're going to get burned! You're going to get burned!"

My house, husband, and the cats are in danger, and I'm the only one here who can do anything about it. I brace myself for the pain and keep going. I go through the foyer and out the door. I fling the heater as far into the yard as I can. Thankfully, I'm not burned.

As I turn around, I see small pieces of plastic burning on the floor. I retrace my steps to the bathroom. I use scatter rugs and anything else I can find to put out the little fires. There are fires on the tile in the foyer, and on the carpet in the living room and hall. There are a few on the tile in the bathroom. I always thought plastic would melt but not burn, but the plastic trash can is in flames.

Once the fires are out, I check in the yard. I see the plastic, that encases the heater, is in flames. I call Jim, and he rushes over. He says he knew it was bad when he saw the heater in flames outside.

I go back to the bathroom. Through the darkness of the smoke, I find the wall where the heater caught on fire. I run my hands over the wall. It's hot, so I throw water on it. I'm having trouble breathing, but I can't stop now. I ask Jim if he can check in the attic for fire. Everything is OK there. Still, I can't rest. I know we won't sleep here until I'm sure the studs inside the walls are cool enough that a fire won't start.

I call the fire department to come out and check the walls for me. While waiting, I wonder why all the doors were open as I removed the heater. It dawns on me that Acy had the frame of mind to open the doors and the storm door. I wouldn't have made it through the house otherwise.

I look for Acy, and he is sitting in the living room. Alan's here now, and he and Jim are sitting with Acy. Acy doesn't seem to have a care in the world and is enjoying the attention.

The firemen arrive and use a meter to check the heat in the walls. They decide everything is all right. Before leaving, they tell me I'm very lucky I wasn't burned. They inform me, the trails of smoke they see underneath my nose indicate I have inhaled too much smoke. They insist I lie down and rest. I'm covered in soot. I go to the bathroom and wash the soot from my face.

I return to the living room to find Jim, Alan, and the firemen gone. I know there will be no rest for me. Soot covers the walls, floors, and furniture. Smoke fills the bedroom. It's hard to see in the bathroom because the smoke is so thick. There is no way we can sleep in this. I use a fan to blow the smoke out the windows, and clean the soot off the floors, furniture, and bathroom fixtures. I decide to wash the ceilings and walls in the bathroom, hall, and bedroom tomorrow. I shower and change clothes. Now I can rest.

I have no idea why the heater caught on fire. I do know that I will never buy a heater encased in plastic again. I will make sure the outside is made of metal, so if something catches fire inside, the whole heater will not go up in flames.

Prescription Medicine

Every evening, Acy's routine is to take his medicine and go to the bedroom. Tonight, he returns for seconds.

"You've taken your medicine for tonight," I say.

"No, I haven't," he insists.

"Yes you did. You can't take any more."

He becomes agitated and aggressive. He grabs a bottle from the shelf. I'm at a point where I have to decide if the risk of suffering an injury is necessary. The thought of him overdosing on his medicine overpowers my fear of traumatization, and a struggling match ensues. I take his medicine from him. I'm surprised how easy it is to wrench the bottle from his hand.

"It's my body. I can do what I want," he says. "I'm single. I don't have to do what you say. Why are you here?"

He can't help it. It's Alzheimer's.

He sulks for a few minutes, but I stand my ground. He stomps back to the bedroom. I move his pills in case he slips back later.

He's up this morning and notices his pills gone. "Where are my pills?"

"I'll put the ones you need each day in a bottle. That way, I'll know when you take them."

He yells, "I'm going to tear this house apart till I find them! I'm moving back home." He's referring to the old home place next door. "I don't want to be treated like a kid."

"Helping someone is not treating them like a kid."

"What makes you think I need your help?"

"The doctor told me to help you."

He doesn't believe me, and slams the cabinet doors while he searches the kitchen. His pills are in a basket sitting on top of the refrigerator. I have read that people afflicted by Alzheimer's never look up. The pills are hidden in plain sight. After a couple weeks, he tires of the search and accepts his bottle of daily pills.

Today, we're going to the doctor for Acy's appointment. We are seated in the car, and I notice he doesn't buckle his seat belt. I remind him, but he doesn't understand. I climb from the car, walk to the other side, and strap him in. From now on, I know I must buckle his seat belt for him. During his visit to the doctor, she gives him a prescription for Seroquel.

"I'm not taking any crazy pills," he says.

Isn't he just a darling?

He struggles with his pills tonight. He wants to chew them up, but he has no teeth or gums because of his cancer surgery. I remind him to take them with water. He asks, "Are your teeth false or real?"

"Real," I answer.

Politely he asks, "Will you chew these up for me?"

I take them to the kitchen and crush them for him.

Bath Time

I pass the bathroom this morning, and I notice Acy bathing at the sink. He's covered in soap, and he's drying himself off. I think maybe he's forgotten where the washcloths are, so I give him one. He takes the cloth and starts drying himself with it. I wonder how I can help him without insulting his dignity. I go over to him and say, "You know, I've always wanted to learn to do that."

He's surprised. "You have?"

"Sure. Will you teach me?"

He proceeds to show me how to bathe him. I follow his instructions. He lets me help with everything but his bottom. He washes this himself. I ask him if I can shampoo his hair. He doesn't care for the idea but agrees reluctantly. He won't step into the shower, so I need to find a way to wash his hair. He can't bend over far enough to use the bathroom sink, so we go to the kitchen. We stand at the faucet, but either I am too short or he's too tall. I need a stool. The hair washing goes well and becomes part of our routine.

A few weeks pass, and he adjusts to me bathing him. It's bath time again, and as he washes his bottom, I say, "Anytime you need help with your bottom, let me know."

"OK." He hands me the washcloth.

"You've already washed today. We'll wait till tomorrow."

The next day, he agrees to let me wash him. I finish, and he says, "Now let me wash yours."

Where did that come from?

Up until now, he hasn't shown any interest in physical contact except for a hug or kiss. I must have triggered a memory.

"I've taken my bath for the day," I reply.

"I'm in love," he announces.

I hug him and give him a kiss. "I love you too," I say. "Let's get you dressed before you freeze."

After I dress him, I step out to run an errand.

I return, and he says, "Faye baby, come over here and sit with me."

We sit and talk for a time.

"Do you know you have a boyfriend?" he asks.

"No. Who is he?"

"It's me."

"I'm glad you're my boyfriend. I'm your girlfriend too."

He puts his arm around my shoulders and pulls me in close, and I feel the light touch of his lips on mine. He asks, "When are we going to get married?"

I'm not falling into this trap. "As soon you find a preacher."

The evening has passed, and we dress for bed. We slide under the covers, and he turns out the light. As the room darkens, I feel him move to my side of the bed. His advances are very awkward and hesitant. I think, *Wait a minute! Wait a minute! This is not going to happen!* I move away, and I try to think what I should do. According to him, we're not married, and I don't think he knows our ages. I tell him, "We can't do that. I might get pregnant."

"That's OK," he says. "We'll keep it and raise it."

Suddenly I'm choking, and I race to the kitchen for some water.

How do I get out of this one? Alzheimer's has changed our roles. I'm no longer his wife, and he is now a curious preteen. Any sexual relationship would make me feel as if I were molesting him. He's too young for me.

When I return to bed, I find him fast asleep. I wonder if I started helping him with his bath too soon.

It's been a few days now, and it appears his poor memory has kicked in. Bathing is once more a daily routine.

I shave and bathe Acy today, and it's time for his pedicure. First I soak his feet. Then he lies on the couch, and I hold his feet in my lap.

He asks, "Are you going to use the pedi file?"

"Now, Acy, if you don't remember anything else, you need to remember this is called a PedEgg."

"It looks like a file to me," says the voice of reason.

He lies back, and the place is quiet while I concentrate on filing his feet.

He breaks the silence. "Why, you're my little girl, aren't you?"

"Yes," I whisper.

Tears fill my eyes as we share the same memory. In the past, whenever he saw me concentrating or looking serious, he would say, "You look like a little girl."

One of the things I miss most is sharing memories with Acy.

I continue working on his feet. As I think about shaving, bathing, and dressing him, I feel as if he has become my little boy.

I finish one foot, and I work on the other. He's getting restless and wants to get up. I distract him by talking to him. "Boy, your feet are a mess. I hope I can get them clean. How did they get in this shape?"

"I don't know." After a few minutes of my babbling and scolding, he interrupts me. "Are we married?"

"Why? Does it sound as if we are?"

"Yes," he replies in a soft voice.

I think, *Odd how, fussing at a man will refresh his memory.*

Delusions: Part Two

Acy's obsessing about his intestines again. He's been this way for three days.

"Dorothy, will you give me something to clean me out?"

I look for the ex-lax boxes filled with M&Ms, but they're gone. "Acy, your bowels moved this morning."

"You're wrong!"

"Let me fix you something to eat."

"I can't. My guts are too full. If I eat, they will burst and get my clothes dirty."

I won't cooperate, and he's angry.

"I will hate you till the day I die!" he says. "I'll get even with you! My cats have more heart than you have!"

I listen in silence. If this is meant to hurt me, he succeeds. *He can't help it. It's Alzheimer's.*

"My guts are so full they are blocking me, keeping me from peeing."

"Do you want me to take you to the hospital?"

"No. Where are my guns?"

He's angry at me and looking for his guns. Thank God they're not in the house.

He's tired and sits down on the couch. He appears to be thinking about something. He looks my way and asks, "Where's Junior?"

"I don't know." *I've been wondering that too.*

His family and friends from his youth call him Junior because his dad's name is Acy Sr.

From this time on, he always refers to himself as "Acy."

Right to Die—Right to Starve

Acy always told me he didn't want to die a lingering death, and he didn't want anything done to extend his life if he ever found himself in that situation. He gave me power of attorney to make all his medical decisions if he no longer can.

Twice this week, while he is lucid and aware of how things are going downhill, he tells me he wishes he were dead. I'm not sure if it's anxiety or if he means it. He refuses to eat or drink liquids. I'm doing everything I can to keep him eating. I know things are going to turn bad at some point, and then

I will have to make the decision to put him in the hospital or let nature take its course.

This morning, he eats a bowl of cereal for breakfast, and I ask, "Do you want a cup of coffee?"

"No, don't make me any more coffee. I never did like it."

This will come as a surprise to many people. As long as I've known Acy, he has always consumed one or two pots of coffee a day. His friends always have a pot of coffee waiting for him when he visits.

The milk in the cereal and water to take pills are the only liquids he consumes now. He refuses to eat or drink the rest of the day. Some days, he goes all day without eating or drinking. I explain the situation to his sister, and she talks with him. She persuades him to eat supper for a couple of days. He hasn't peed in two days. We visit Jim and Bessie, and Acy is engaged in conversation for about two hours. This makes him thirsty. Bessie asks, "Would you like a cup of coffee?" She takes a drink from her bottle of water.

"What are you drinking?" he asks.

"Bottled water."

"I want that."

"OK."

He drinks two pint bottles of water.

We leave for home, but he refuses to drink more water. Late that evening I call Bessie, and she brings her bottled water. She coaxes him into drinking more water. She leaves, and a few hours later, he pees.

We get a good night's sleep, and the next day, he pees twice. Again, his only meal for the day is a bowl of cereal.

When he was in his thirties, he was diagnosed as anorexic. He never had an appetite, never got hungry, and ate only because he knew he had to. I wonder if he has forgotten he needs to eat, and without an appetite, he no longer understands the importance of eating and drinking. I try to tell him but can't get through to him.

Three Hospitals in One Week

Acy wants to go to the hospital. Since he isn't eating or drinking, I think I should take him. His hospital of choice is fifty miles away. It's the one he frequents, so I agree to take him there.

All his tests come back normal. It turns out, all he needs is three cups of liquid a day. With his milk and water to take pills, he's been drinking that much most days. He's over 6'2", and weighed 190 pounds five weeks ago. Now he weighs 167.

He's released, and we're on the way home. He asks, "Why did we go to the hospital?"

"You asked me to take you because you were sick."

"Oh, I didn't do that. You're wrong," he says.

"If you say so."

Three days later, he asks me to drive him to the hospital again. I try to talk him out of it, but he heads out the door in his underwear, and he's walking in the road. I can't get him to listen to me, so I agree to his demands. This time, I take him to a hospital closer to home.

I tell the doctor what's going on, and he runs tests, which come back normal. He notices Acy's spitting cup and wants to know if Acy chews tobacco. I tell him no. I explain Acy's been doing this for close to two years. The doctor observes him for a few minutes, and Acy sits quietly. The doctor confirms that spitting is caused by Alzheimer's. He says Acy forgets how to swallow.

He's released, and on the way home, he asks, "Why did you take me there?"

I don't bother to give him an answer.

Two days later, he's ready to go again. "Will you drive me to the hospital? It's a matter of life and death."

"I don't know how to get to the hospital."

"I'll find someone to take me."

Sure enough, he crosses the heavily traveled road and goes to the neighbors' house. They don't answer the door, so he walks up and down in the road and stops long enough to knock on doors.

No one answers, so he comes back. "Will you drive me to the hospital?"

"I don't know how to get to the hospital."

"I'll find someone to take me."

He runs in and out of the house and up and down the road. He locks himself out of the house several times. He can't remember we have a back door, so he tries kicking in the front door. I try to get him to leave the door open, but he keeps locking it. I put tape on the latch, but he pulls it off.

He rages, "I hate you! I hope you rot in hell! You are driving me crazy! Don't you feel guilty? What would my dad think of you now for the way you're treating me?"

My first thought is, *He would thank me for trying to take care of you.* His dad was always my best advocate.

"Will you drive me to the hospital?"

"I don't know how to get to the hospital."

"Then I'll walk."

He storms out of the house and heads for the road. The closest hospital is twenty miles away, and he's already been there. He's walking in the middle of the road. I go out and try to persuade him to come back home. "Acy, it's a long way to the hospital. It will take too long to walk there. Why don't you come back home? Will you let me fix you something to eat?" He ignores me. "You're not supposed to walk in the road. It's against the law. They could drive by, pick you up, and put you in jail." He moves to the side of the road. I tell him,

"I have to go back to the house. I need to go to the bathroom."

He turns and follows me home.

I've taken him to two hospitals, and neither would keep him. I've never been in this position, and I don't know anyone who has. I don't know what to do for someone when their mind snaps.

He's getting aggressive at this point. He starts pulling on me and my blouse to try to make me take him to the hospital. I tell him he's hurting me, and he stops for a while.

I call Jack. He arrives and distracts Acy. He placates Acy for a while. Acy sits quietly on the steps, and I sit with him. He doesn't say much, and it appears his rampage is over. As soon as Jack leaves, Acy becomes agitated again.

I talk him into going in the house. We enter the house, and before I can stop him, he turns and runs out the door. He walks up and down the side of the road for an hour. He returns to the house covered in sweat. He hasn't had anything to eat or drink all day.

"Let me get you some water," I say.

"I don't want any."

I go to the kitchen to get a glass of water and a Seroquel pill. I return to the living room. "Here's your medicine."

He takes the pill and goes back to the road.

When he comes back, he's panting and puffing. "Please sit down and rest," I say.

"I don't want to." He has lost his voice and speaks in a whisper.

"Let me get you a glass of water."

"I don't want any."

"Honey, you haven't had anything to eat or drink today. At least let me fix you something to eat."

"No! I've got willpower," he says, and out the door he goes.

I never dreamed he could keep going at this pace. He's been rampaging since 7:00 a.m. It's now 2:00 p.m.

Acy doesn't care for the VA hospital. Still, I do the one thing he would never agree to. I have no choice but to call them. I've taken him everywhere else. My only chance is maneuvering him into the VA hospital without him recognizing where we are.

I explain that I'm taking him to another hospital. The drive is an hour and a half, but he's content all the way there. There are signs along the route directing me to the hospital. I glance at him, but he doesn't notice the signs. When we pull in, I see the hospital name written in giant letters on the front of the building. My hands are shaking, and I hold my breath as I drive by the door. He speaks for the first time. "Haven't I been here before?"

With a voice calmer than I feel, I say, "I don't know."

I park and hope for the best as I guide him into the emergency room.

They admit him immediately. I explain the situation to the doctor, and tell him about my concerns for Acy's safety because of his obsession with the road. I mention that it's not safe for anyone that tries to coax him out of the road. It's possible he could shove that person in front of a car. At last, I've found a doctor who understands. The doctor pages the social worker, but she's left for the day. He offers to keep Acy overnight, so I can return home for some rest, and come back the next day.

Acy's asking for something to eat. He hasn't eaten all day, and supper has already been served at the hospital. I'm afraid they won't feed him. I want to take him home and make sure he has something to eat. I decide to bring him back tomorrow.

It's after dark, and we arrive home about 10:00 p.m. I fix Acy something to eat, take care of the cats, wash the dishes, and help Acy to bed. I'm trying to help him with his medication, and I feel sick. I'm dizzy to the point of passing out. I don't want to fall and hurt myself, so I lie down on the floor. After several tries, I manage to climb into bed. I tell him he will have to take his pills by himself.

It's morning, and the pills are still there. I ask him if he wants to go to the hospital. He refuses. He says he needs to rest today.

The social worker calls in the afternoon to help me decide on a nursing home. She offers to keep him at the hospital until placement. I hesitate to make a decision. He's slept all day. I want to see if he has calmed down some. She offers an aide, three times a week, and I accept.

If he doesn't calm down, I will have to place him for his own safety. Do I feel guilty? Yes. After all, I did tell him he would always have a home here.

Another day dawns. At six thirty, Acy wakes me. He's fully dressed. He says, "I need to go to the hospital."

"OK, but I have to get ready first."

Out the door he goes. He walks up and down the road and knocks on doors. He's yells, "Somebody help me! I need to go to the hospital! It's a matter of life and death!"

No one answers the door. He continues while I prepare to leave.

When I'm ready to leave, I find Acy walking the road. While I'm talking him out of the road, I notice someone has broken the chain across the drive of our detached garage. I don't have time for this now. I help Acy into the car, and we start our long drive to the hospital.

After we arrive, I tell the social worker I have no choice but to put him in a nursing home. Since he's sitting there listening, she becomes worried he may get upset. She asks me to call her when we get home, so we can work out arrangements.

We leave the hospital, and half way home, I suggest, "Find us a CD we can listen to."

A light flickers in his eyes. "CD?"

Oh crap! I've said the wrong thing. Now he's thinking of his CD in the bank.

"The next thing I want you to do is take me to the bank to get my money," he announces.

"I need to stop at the store to buy some cat food first."

"Those cats don't need any food. You take me to the bank."

I pull into the store's parking lot and say, "I won't be but a minute."

When I return, he's squirming in his seat. "Let's go! You shouldn't have stopped here."

I drive down the road, and he pulls at my clothes. "Acy, don't do that. I'm trying to drive."

He uses his finger and jabs me in the ribs. He continues for sixteen miles until we arrive home.

I pull in the drive. As we get out of the car, Jim and Acy's sister cross the road. Jim's anxious, and his voice breaks, as he says, "We've been looking for you all day. I noticed the chain that crosses your drive was broken, and called the police. I thought Acy may have harmed you and then broke the chain leaving."

"No. That was broken before we left for the hospital."

Jim informs me, "Well, Jack showed up and called the station. He got permission to kick your door in to make sure you were all right. He wasn't successful, so he left."

Jim is referring to the garage attached to our home. They were trying to kick in the garage entrance door, but Acy always keeps a wooden bolt across it. I check the door for damage. I find the frame is broken, and the metal door is warped. I see footprints in the middle of the door. I have neither the time nor energy to deal with this at the moment. The bolt will hold for now.

Acy has plans of his own. "Come on. Let's go to the bank!"

I refuse to get in the car. "No. I need to go to the bathroom."

The social worker is waiting for my call, so I'm trying to maneuver my way into the house to call her. I make it into the house and start down the hall before he catches up with me.

"Take me to the bank!"

I turn and walk back through the house with him, but manage to put the social worker's phone number in my pocket.

Once outside, he becomes aggressive and starts pulling me down the drive. Jim steps between us, and Acy loses his grip. Jim tries to distract him, but Acy steps around him, grabs me, and starts pulling on me again. Jim places his arms around Acy, and I pull free.

Acy's sister tells him, "The bank is closed now."

"That's all right. We'll be down there when it opens in the morning."

He grabs for me, and I walk down the road with him, hoping he will grow tired and change his mind. After we walk about five hundred feet, I lose my patience and jerk my arm free. "I've had enough of this. I'm going back home!"

I know it isn't safe to turn my back on him, but I'm angry and too tired to care. I walk back up the road, and he follows.

I need to call the social worker before she leaves for the day. I start up the steps and hear Acy tell Jim, "I'll make it worth your while if you take me to the bank."

Acy sees me slip into the house. He runs and catches up with me. He gets a strong grip on me and pulls me toward the door.

Jim sees what's happening and rushes through the door. He manages to hold Acy. As Acy pulls, the three of us are locked arm in arm, and we dance toward the door. We reach the door, and Acy loosens his grip on me. Jim falls out the door and takes Acy with him. Jim holds Acy back long enough for me to make it to the bedroom and lock the door.

A thunderous noise fills the room. It sounds like lightning is striking the door. I call the social worker, and with Acy in the background beating on the door, I tell her what's happening. She instructs me to call 911 and ask them to bring him back to the hospital. Jack picks up the 911 call. Though he's off duty, he stops by.

Acy sees him in the driveway, recognizes him, and grins. He approaches Jack with the offer of a handshake. Jack offers his hand. Instead of shaking it, Acy pulls on Jack's arm. Being a law officer, Jack stands rigid. Everyone watches and knows Acy is testing Jack to see if he can take him. Jack's hand never moves. After several attempts, Acy pulls his hand away, and he and Jack enter the house for a visit.

Jack tries to discourage me from sending Acy back to the hospital. He tells me he doesn't know how to drive there. I assume he is referring to taking Acy there himself. I tell him, it's all right. He can follow me. I use a map.

Acy and Jack return to the driveway as two deputies drive up.

Acy races through the house looking for me. "I think I made a mistake! I think I made a mistake!"

It's too late. I can't help him now.

He rushes back to Jack. "I think I made a mistake! I think I made a mistake!"

Jack talks to the deputies and returns to the house to talk to me. He's worried the deputies are too young and inexperienced to know how to handle Acy and may end up hurting him. Therefore, Jack calls for an ambulance. It arrives, and Acy refuses to enter the ambulance. I stay in the kitchen. I'm afraid it might make things worse if he sees me. Finally, he's in the ambulance, and I talk to the paramedics. I'm told, if he doesn't calm down, they will stop at the local hospital for medicine. The deputies stay until the ambulance leaves with Acy, and I follow the ambulance.

Hospital Admission

We arrive at the hospital, and they're expecting us. Acy is admitted to the hospital, and they run tests. The doctor says the tests they ran two days ago came back normal. Today, they show kidney failure and dehydration. They give him an IV. They will keep him here until he is placed. I no longer trust him. I wouldn't be able to sit, lie down, or turn my back on him. I tell the doctor he was only aggressive with me. They're going to evaluate him and put him on the appropriate medicine to help with his delusions.

It's too late for me to try to make the trip home. A clerk at the admission desk helps me find a place to spend the night. I'm not familiar with the streets here. I'm uncomfortable driving on them in the dark, so the clerk calls me a cab.

It's morning, and the clerk at the hotel's front desk calls me a cab. I ride back to the hospital.

I step off the elevator and see Acy. He's sitting at the nurses' station down the hall. He's in a wheel-chair with a tray across the front. This restrains him from walking. I ask one of the staff to remove the tray so he can walk with me.

I help him eat and spend time with him. When he gets sleepy, I'm ready to leave for home. So is he. I tell him I have to go find a place to eat. I give him a kiss and whisper, "I love you."

"I know it. You always did."

At least he knows he's loved.

During his stay here at the VA hospital, everyone has been kind to me and giving me lots of hugs. It occurs to me I must look as if I need a hug. I think Acy needs one too. He doesn't know where he is or why he can't come home. When I visit, I shave and bathe him. I stay long enough to feed him two meals. When he takes a nap, I leave.

They have adjusted his medicine, and he is re-laxed and peaceful. They have also declared him incompetent. They say he is self-oriented and not aware of anyone else. While sitting with him, he sur-prises me. "I can see the pain in your face."

He's always been able to look at my face and know what I'm feeling. I'm beginning to think he's aware of those around him but is losing his ability to respond.

CHAPTER 6
2009: PART TWO

Nursing Home Number One

The VA locates a nursing home, and the social worker sets a time for an interview with the nursing home's representative. We gather in Acy's room so the representative can meet Acy. Everything goes well, but I mention what I feel could be a drawback. The social worker and I explain Acy's obsession with his clothes. I tell the representative that when Acy goes to the bathroom for a bowel movement, he pulls his clothes off before he enters the bathroom, and leaves them outside the bathroom door so they won't get dirty. The social worker agrees. The representative doesn't feel this will be a problem, and everyone is in agreement for him to be admitted to the nursing home.

My next stop is the nursing home to admit him. I finish the paperwork and step into the hall. I watch him enter through the front doors. He appears fine, so I don't approach him. One of the nursing home's staff says it may be easier for him if he doesn't see me leave, so I return home without telling him good-bye.

I arrive to an empty house and wonder how I will adjust to living alone. This is like dealing with death. Everything is out of my control. I have no desire to live here without Acy. I miss him more than I could have imagined. The loneliness is unbearable. There's no hope. There's only waiting. For what, I'm not sure. The quietness of the house is ear shattering. I miss the sound of my own voice. There was always a stream of chatter between us. I begin to cry, and Jim finds me this way. He takes me home with him. He listens while I talk and cry until there are no more tears. I assure him I'm OK, and he lets me go back to my house.

My first night home alone, there are heavy rains, and the roads are flooded. I wait for the roads to be cleared and call daily to check on Acy. I'm told he's doing fine, and he sounds all right when I talk to him. When the roads allow, I visit him. He likes the certified nurse assistant they have assigned to him. When I arrive, Acy and the CNA are deep in conversation. Acy is telling him about one of the adventures from his past and the CNA is laughing. Acy is relaxed and smiling and I think he's adjusting.

I receive a call from the nursing home. They tell me Acy took his clothes off, and they sent him back to the VA hospital for a behavioral evaluation. I call the hospital, and I'm told their evaluation shows nothing out of the ordinary. They return him to the nursing home, and I receive a letter from them. They have set up a meeting to discuss their problem with Acy.

The next day, I visit with him until they call us into the room where the meeting is held. We're informed that Acy's ritual with his clothing is unacceptable because of the female residents in the home. They give no reason why the representative agreed to this during the interview at the VA hospital. They say he must be put on probation. I can't grasp the concept of putting someone who has been declared mentally incompetent on probation. They place him on their one-on-one care for a week to help him adjust. We return to his room, and a staff member stops by and tells me she enjoys his company. She says she sits with him and talks to him from time to time.

I report back to the VA hospital social worker, and she tells me she also talked to the nursing home representative. The social worker informs me, she explained Acy's clothing ritual to the representative after they left his room, and the representative had given her approval.

It's June 9, 2009. Today is our thirty-fourth wedding anniversary. I buy Acy a card full of verses of love. I enter his room at the nursing home and hand him the card. He shows no interest in the card or our anniversary. As I start to read out loud, I'm forced to accept that I'm alone. I see him lying on the bed before me, but I'm alone. I go to bed at night alone and wake up alone. I handle all that life places before me alone. I no longer have the support of a husband. There won't be any more long talks. Alzheimer's has stolen all this from me. *I hate Alzheimer's.*

The staff follows a routine for caring for the residents. Acy was agreeable at first, but now he refuses to be bathed. I decide to see if he will let me bathe him. "Let's get your clothes together and take a bath."

"You're not going to turn that cold water on me, are you?"

"I promise you, I'll bathe you the way you want to be bathed."

I take him to the sink and give him his bath. At times, I find myself bathing him during our visits.

A nursing home staff member states that Acy needs someone to stay with him every day. I observe his behavior, but I can't understand some of their complaints. They tell me he is a different person when I'm there.

Not only has Acy's story telling ceased but now he says very little and only answers in short words. Every time I visit, he begs me to take him home. He begs me to marry him. He thinks if we're married I'll have to let him come home with me.

When I visit, it's three hours round trip to the nursing home. Around ten o'clock, I eat breakfast at McDonald's. I then go to the home and stay with Acy until 6:00 p.m. I make sure he eats lunch and supper. By then, I'm ready to find a fast-food restaurant. I am aware this is not healthy, but I have trouble concentrating on myself.

Acy's ability to walk causes problems for the staff at the nursing home. Only a few residents are wheelchair free. The complaint is, that he's going in the women's room, and it scares them. Some of the residents are there because of physical disabilities, and they approach me about their experiences.

One male resident is there because of a heart disability. He tells me Acy walks constantly because he can't find his room. He finally gets so tired he goes into any room to lie down on the bed. The resident says Acy lies on his bed, but he doesn't mind if it's not in use.

Another resident with a heart disability relates to me her experience. She tells me, "I was in bed late one evening, and Acy came into my room and began pulling off his shoes. I told him, 'No, no. You can't stay here.' I noticed he was having trouble getting his shoes on, so I patted the foot of the bed and told him, 'Come over here, baby, and I'll help you with your shoes.' I helped him put his shoes on, and he went back into the hall and started walking again."

Because he walks and tries to get out the door, he wears an ankle bracelet that locks the front door. He figures out how to throw their locks. He holds the lever down on the door for fifteen seconds, and the door releases. It upsets me to think he can walk out the door that easily. The staff talks about how smart he is. I don't know why people can't understand. He's not stupid. It's Alzheimer's.

We visit, but I'm distracted by the fact that things are going downhill. He sees the concern on my face. "I know something's bothering you. What is it?"

I wonder how someone so self-oriented can be so aware. Maybe if I look a little closer, I can find glimpses of him.

Acy isn't adjusting to the nursing home, and the staff isn't adjusting to him. I'm getting an uneasy feeling I have placed him too soon. I have no idea what action I should take. There is no way I can be there every day, and the time comes when I get the call. I'm told there has been an incident, and after two months, Acy has been sent back to the VA hospital because of resistive behaviors. They say he needs one-on-one care, and they aren't staffed for that kind of care. *Thank God.* I feel this solution, is a relief for all of us. I return long enough to collect his belongings. It's not always true that a nursing home can provide better care. At Acy's expense, I learned this the hard way.

Returned to VA Hospital

I have no idea what to expect when I enter the VA hospital. I find Acy in a wheelchair with a tray.

I sneak a kiss, but he seems distracted. His head is lowered and tilted to one side. I ask, "What's wrong?"

His eyes plead with me. He motions for me to lean in toward him. I lean over, and he says, "I pissed on myself."

It's evident he's too embarrassed to tell the nice strangers.

I locate his CNA and tell him about Acy's predicament. The CNA takes him to his room to change his underwear. Acy's wearing pull-up protective undershorts. Before the CNA puts clean shorts on him, he wants to know if Acy needs to use the bathroom. "Do you need to go pee?" Acy's unresponsive. "Do you need to go pee?"

Still no answer. The CNA continues to repeat the question.

I look Acy in the eye and say, "Do you need to piss?"

"Yes," he answers.

I look at the CNA and say, "He thinks pee is a letter in the alphabet." The CNA dresses him. I say, "He won't be needing the wheelchair while I'm here."

At the end of the day, I let the staff know I'm leaving.

Some of the CNAs remember him from the last time, when he was at the other end of the hall. They remember when we walked the halls, because it set their alarms off.

They attach an alarm to his bed. It sounds when the bed is empty. This is used at night to alert them. This way, he doesn't walk unsupervised in the hall.

After observing him a few days, the VA doctors say they can't see any behavioral problems. They say he's always quiet. Even though he always begged to go home when he stayed at the nursing home, he's content here and never asks to go home. He's given a job sorting papers. He talks more now, and can form simple sentences in order to talk with the VA hospital staff.

I meet with the social worker to decide Acy's future. Their long term ward is full. She mentions placing him in another nursing home. I plead with her to let me take him home. She agrees and offers to help me any way she can.

When I visit Acy at the hospital, I always take him to the bathroom. He pulls the elastic leg of his protective underwear over, and pees through the leg. He hates the underwear and tries to remove it. I tell him he has to wear it while he's in the hospital because they can't find his other underwear. The CNA tells me Acy hasn't had a bowel movement yet. I'm on the lookout for that event.

The doctor wants me to arrive at the hospital early one day so he can talk to me about adjusting Acy's medicine before he's discharged. He will be seeing a different doctor at the clinic. I hope he doesn't want to change the medicine. For some reason, they all seem to want to do this.

It's time to take him home. I gather his belongings, and Acy interrupts me. "I need to use the bathroom."

I take him to the bathroom, but this time he pulls down his pants. It seems the event we've all been waiting for has arrived. While his britches are down, he refuses to pull the underwear back up.

"Acy, please pull them up. You only have to wear them for a few more hours."

"OK. If it makes you happy."

Indeed it does.

I spot Acy's CNA in the hall and give him the good news. I know he will want to put Acy's bowel movement on record. Hospitals are like that.

It's time to leave, and we walk to the elevator. The staff has gotten so used to seeing us walk the halls, they forget the traditional "wheelchair to the car" routine. Acy hesitates to enter the elevator, so I say, "Come on. Let's go." He stands firm. A staff member steps off the elevator. I say, "He doesn't want to leave."

The staff member turns toward Acy. "Hey buddy, this is a nice place to visit, but you don't want to live here. Right?"

"Yes."

"She comes over here most days to visit you. That's a lot of traveling."

I chime in. "Well, he's worth it."

The staff member asks Acy, "Wouldn't you like to go home?"

"Yes."

"She wants to take you home. Isn't that nice?"

"Yes."

"If you'll go with her, she'll take you home. It'll be OK. You'll be all right."

Acy studies my face. "OK," he says and enters the elevator.

Home Again

We make it to the car and settle in for the long ride home. He can no longer carry on a conversation. I think better of asking for a CD. This time, I turn on the radio.

He no longer recognizes the route we're taking home. When we're halfway there, I decide to reassure him that we're still on the road home. "I traveled this road most days to visit you."

To my surprise, he speaks for the first time. "Well I'm worth it."

With laughter in my throat and tears in my eyes, I say, "You sure are, baby. You sure are."

I now know, not only can he can hear and understand, sometimes he even remembers.

We arrive home, and we're getting out of the car. Acy recognizes home and is giddy with happiness. Bessie and Jim see us pull in, and they cross the road to greet Acy. Jim reaches him first, hugs him, and tells him, "We sure are glad you're home."

Bessie walks up the drive and asks sympathetically, "How are you feeling?"

Acy puts on his Jack Benny deadpan face and says, "With my fingers."

Bessie is speechless, and Jim laughs as if Jack himself has taken the floor. A smile spreads across Acy's face. He realizes his joke was a success.

With the welcome-home party in full swing, the social worker from the VA calls to see how things are going. She says if I have any problems to call 911 and tell them to bring him back.

Bessie and Jim leave, and I put the deadbolt rule into action. I'll always wear the key around my neck. "You need to have a key made for me," he announces.

Earlier I mentioned locks, and he said locks were useless because anyone can take down the door by removing the pins. He seems to have forgotten this.

Acy goes to the bathroom, and I hand him a pair of his regular undershorts. I shop on the Internet and find washable incontinence briefs. These are made like regular briefs, except they're padded. He has no problem with them. I feel this will make the transition easier when he needs the disposable underwear.

He's now eating every two hours and gaining four pounds a week. Everyone says he looks, walks, and talks better. The folding commode chair, walker, and wheelchair the VA gave him sit idle for now. They will be there when he needs them. Everyone says he's doing this well because of my determination.

I've been lucky. I know at any time my health could fail. If anything should happen to me, plans are made for him to be placed in a nursing home. I'm trying to cover all bases for his care.

Since returning home, Acy refuses to bathe or let me help him. I put his clothing ritual to good use. I wait until he pulls off his clothes to go to the bathroom. As soon as he closes the door, I race down the hall and grab his clothes. I replace them with the clean ones I keep close by. Clean clothes will do until I can convince him to bathe.

He loves to visit with Bessie and Jim. I drop whatever I'm doing when he wants to visit. He constantly yells, "Let's go."

We work out a compromise. I tell him he's too dirty to go out in public. He decides it's all right to let me bathe him.

Today, we visit with Bessie and Jim, and Acy's sister stops by. Someone mentions the bank, and Acy informs them he has a CD there. The subject is changed, but it's too late. After we return home, he announces, "Dorothy, I want my money."

"Your CD hasn't matured."

This satisfies him for a while, but he keeps bringing up the money. I give him money at times to placate him.

Every day I help him shave and bathe. As a reward, we go to Wendy's for a Frosty. Afterward, we go to Walmart. We shop and do a lot of walking in the store. I consider this his physical therapy to keep him ambulatory. On the way home, if he sees the Wendy's sign, we stop for another Frosty.

Acy develops an odd behavior. He talks to people who aren't there. When we return home from Wendy's today, Acy lies down to rest. His eyes are shut, but he's not asleep, He starts to talk. I realize he isn't talking to me. I listen, but I can't figure out who he's talking to. This goes on the rest of the day.

Among other sounds, he hears voices, music, and a phone ringing. Still, he seems highly alert. He appears to get better and worse at the same time. After he visits with Jim this evening, I have a little talk with Jim. He tells me he's noticed the same thing. He says one minute Acy is alert and talking rationally, and the next he isn't making any sense at all.

He lies on the couch today, and suddenly he's dodging aircraft. "Look out! That plane is too low."

This continues for about five minutes.

I try to figure out what changes have been made to his schedule. The only thing I can think of, is a change in his medicine. After studying his list of medicines, I stop the new one, and the problem disappears.

VA Doctor's Appointment

Acy has a setback when he starts seeing a doctor from the VA as an outpatient. Jim goes with us for Acy's first appointment. Acy's doctor at the VA implies that Acy's PTSD should no longer be a problem because of his dementia. The doctor's wrong. He's about to discover this for himself.

Acy meets the doctor. Without introduction, the doctor starts immediately throwing questions at Acy. This causes Acy to become confused. Dementia keeps him from knowing the difference between brown-skinned males with black hair. He thinks they are all the enemy. He thinks the doctor is Vietnamese. He runs from the room, and the doctor calls the security guard.

Once Acy's in the waiting room, Jim catches him.

"The government made us fight the Viet Cong, and now they hire them as doctors. I'm going to get the car and run over him," he tells Jim.

By the time the security guard arrives, Acy has calmed down. While Acy stays with Jim, I talk to the doctor. I explain that in Acy's eyes, he is North Vietnamese. "Because the US government taught Acy they are the enemy," I say, "he now sees you as the enemy."

The doctor decides not to pursue this visit any further. He sets him up another appointment. This time, Acy sees a different doctor. His visit is with a Caucasian female doctor. She begins questioning him calmly, and he's responsive. Then she asks, "Are you married?"

"No."

She points to me. "Who is this?"

"Dorothy."

She becomes aggressive. "What's she to you?"

His face reddens. He repositions himself in the chair as if he is about to pounce. She notices the anger in his eyes and says he's becoming agitated. She drops the line of questioning.

I remember him telling me that we would live together and say we were married. If I know him, and I think I do, he thinks she's being too nosy. He's always been a private person, and believes his personal life is no one else's business. He remains calm through the rest of the visit.

When we return home, curiosity overwhelms me. I want to know what he was thinking at the doctor's office. We settle in for the evening. I ask, "What am I to you?"

"You're the one I love on."

There you go. He may have dementia, but he still knows he has a right to his own privacy. After all, he's never been a believer in kiss-and-tell.

He has another appointment with his regular doctor. The doctor ceases to be aggressive, and he doesn't have any problems at his follow-up visits. It's clear that when someone is aggressive with Acy, he responds with aggression. This is not caused by Alzheimer's. This has always been one of his traits.

Susie

Susie is one of Acy's home aides. Today is her first day, and I'm concerned about bath time. Since he's only recently started allowing me to bathe him again, I'm worried about how he will react to her.

The first thing I do is tell her about the ritual with his clothes. I tell her he can strip naked in his own home if he wants. If this is a problem, I understand her seeking a client elsewhere. It turns out she is very professional and flexible to her clients' needs. She's accommodating, and he has no problem letting her bathe and shave him.

He seldom speaks, so when it's time for her to leave, we're surprised when he asks, "What do I owe you?"

"You don't owe me anything. I've already been paid."

He turns to me and asks, "Have you been paid too?"

I lean in for a kiss and say, "I have now."

The VA social worker tells me that while the aide is caring for Acy, I should use that time to catch up on errands outside the home. Susie has been here long enough to be comfortable, and Acy gets along with her, so I decide it's time for me to venture out.

I'm dressed and ready to tackle some errands. I scurry around to look for my keys and purse, and from across the room, I hear, "You sure are pretty."

I look to see if someone has entered the room, then I glance toward Acy. There he is. He's over six foot two with eyes of blue. He has a tender smile on his face. He says, "I love you, Faye baby."

How did I ever get so lucky? The force of love draws me toward him. I say, "Thank you, baby. I love you too."

As I slip into his arms, I'm carried backward in time. He kisses me, and it leaves me wanting more.

The sound of the doorbell reminds me that Alzheimer's reigns as king around here. I open the door, and as Susie enters, I tell Acy I have a few errands to run. He wants to go with me, but I tell him he has to stay with Susie.

"Are you going to be gone long?"

"I'll be back as quick as I can."

"Well, hurry back. I don't like it here without you."

"I'll do my very best." I steal one last kiss, and I move toward the door.

I hurry to finish my errands and return home. Susie rushes to meet me at the door. She says, "He talked to me! He talked to me! He asked if I'm married and whether I have children."

Until now, she has never heard Acy carry on a conversation.

Acy's doing things he previously forgot how to do, such as using the TV remote. He hasn't been able to use the remote for over four months. He's regained some of his vocabulary and is now able to join in on simple conversations. Everyone makes sure he's included in activities. Susie has been here for four weeks, and he can now call her by name. This makes me want to dance a jig. Who says Alzheimer's patients can't learn new things? I know this is temporary, but it's a blessing to be cherished.

Susie's worked here two months. She finds a more productive job in another state. I bring Frostys home to celebrate Susie's new job. Acy tells her she's been like a member of the family.

VA Home Visit

Acy's new aide, Alice, will be arriving soon to shave and help Acy with his bath. Her boss is coming for a review. The VA is sending someone to see if I'm competent enough to handle Acy's VA checks. The VA won't accept a power of attorney. Alice arrives first and shaves Acy. She takes him to the bathroom for his bath.

The VA representative arrives and starts to interview me. We sit down at the kitchen table, and I'm answering her questions. I hear Alice scream.

"Dorothy! There's something wrong with Acy!"

I rush to the bathroom, and as I pass, I grab my office chair with wheels. I enter the bathroom and notice Acy is having trouble standing. I move the chair close to him. I tell him, "Acy honey, lean on me. He collapses in my arms. I use my leg to swivel the chair around and ease him into the chair.

The representative is observing and says, "This is the time when you need his wheelchair."

"Show me where there is room to fit that monstrosity of a wheelchair in this small space."

I move Acy from the bathroom to the living room. The representative agrees that a swiveling chair with arms and wheels is best for a tight fit. I start to place him on the couch, but Alice says, "He needs to be on the floor."

"All right, but you'll have to be prepared to help lower him to the floor."

The representative holds the chair, so I can lift him out.

We have no idea Acy has recovered some his strength. I lift him out of the chair, and he's on his feet. He walks across the floor and sits down on the couch. We stand there, speechless. My hands are shaking as I call for an ambulance. It's not in this area. I'm not familiar with the route they are taking, so I pass the phone to Alice. She gives them directions. The ambulance arrives with the paramedics, but their blood pressure monitor doesn't work, so they use mine. He refuses their assistance.

"I don't need the ambulance," he says. "All I need is a Frosty."

He's not giving up his reward for bathing. The mood in the room lightens, and after examining him, the paramedics leave.

Next, Alice's supervisor arrives, and she examines Acy. While Alice and the supervisor discuss business, the VA representative continues to interview me. The representative says that the total of my expenses are more than Acy's VA check. Our other income will cover the rest. Everyone leaves, and we're off to Wendy's for a Frosty.

Now that Acy's VA check is secured, I no longer worry about checks bouncing. I give him an allowance. On rare occasions, he goes with me to the bank. Since he knows it's for him, he sits and waits patiently. This stops his obsession about money. He likes to shop at Walmart. I don't ask what he does with his money. It's his, and he does what he wants with it.

Move to the Bedroom

Acy turns mean-spirited. He can hardly walk or talk, but he still tries to be controlling. His need to control takes on a life of its own. Once more, he focuses on the air conditioner. He refuses to let me turn it on. He goes to bed, and I turn it on. He gets back up and lies down on the couch. He says the air conditioner is too cold and demands I turn it off. I turn it off, and two minutes later, he goes back to bed. The air conditioner has a safety feature and won't turn back on for a while.

He decides to sleep on the couch and wants the TV turned off. I turn it off and watch the one in the bedroom. He shows up and tells me to move over so we can watch together. The next night, he announces he's sleeping on the couch. The air conditioner and TV are turned off, and I'm reading. It's around 8:00 p.m., and still daylight. He wants the light turned off. He drives me out of the living room. I move my rocker to the bedroom and return for my laptop and earphones.

As I settle in, I look up. There he is in the doorway. He throws himself onto the bed. "I guess you think I am doing the opposite."

I don't speak. I'm too busy taking deep breaths and counting to one hundred. I don't ask him the opposite of what. I'm too tired to care. I get up and leave the room. *He can't help it. It's Alzheimer's.*

Bessie drops by for a visit. Acy returns to the living room and asks, "Don't you think it's time to go home and go to bed?"

I thank God she understands. I'm thinking the doctor was right. I am a prisoner in my own home. I talk to his doctor, and he makes a medicine adjustment.

A Day in the Life

It's October, and our days have evolved into a routine. It's not one you would expect, but a routine just the same. Acy wants to go for a ride. First, he wants to stop at Wendy's for a Frosty. The next stop is Walmart. As we enter the store, he's close behind me. It's easier for him to follow me than walk beside me. In the store, I turn to my left to get a cart. When I turn around, he's gone. I watch for him while I pick up a couple of things in the front. There's still no sign of him, so I check out. No one's around to call him to the service desk. He wouldn't be able to find the desk anyway. If I can't find him soon, I'll alert the store's staff. I decide to start looking for him at the car, and there he stands. I ask him where he's been. It turns out, when I turned left, he made a right to the bathrooms, and then returned to the car. I'm surprised he knew where the car was. Half the time, I can't remember where I park. How can someone in the advanced stages of Alzheimer's (according to the doctor) be able to do this, but can't button his shirt? This is the mystery of Alzheimer's.

We return to the store to finish shopping. I notice he's not carrying his spit cup. I hurry toward the aisle where the cups are. When we get there, I open a pack of cups and give him one. I pay for the pack when we are ready to leave.

We're on the road once more, but he has to stop at Wendy's for another Frosty. We stop for gas and then head home.

I want to wash and wax the car, but now I am running late. While he naps, Bessie helps me so I can finish before dark. I go to her home to show her something on the computer. I'm there half an hour, and darkness moves in. He charges through the door and demands to know if I am going to bed anytime that night. We go home, but he refuses to go to bed. He turns on the TV and I turn on the computer. He complains because I went next door. He starts pacing back and forth behind my back. Since I'm not sure what's on his mind, I shut down the desktop. I get my laptop and go to the bedroom. He leaves the house and goes next door. I decide to turn the TV on and watch the Sprint Cup races. Acy and I used to do this together. He returns and changes the channel. I reach my limit. I tell him the TV will remain on the races, and he can go watch the TV in his bedroom. He thinks for a minute, lays down the remote, and watches the races with me. *He can't help it. It's Alzheimer's.* I give him his medicine, and he's quiet the rest of the night. I think, *Welcome to our world.*

Halloween

As Halloween draws near, Acy's excited. He wants to dress up and go next door to the neighbors' house, and his sister's house. I use an old wig and long housecoat to make him a costume. I call to let the neighbors know he's coming. I tell them to get their camera ready. I fight the urge to hold his hand as he crosses the road. I watch from the living room window to make sure he's safe. His first stop is Jim and Bessie's. He leaves their home and stops at his sister's house. Bessie calls to tell me they were able to take pictures, and he beamed from all the attention. She says, as they moved toward the couch, she looked up at him and noticed his shy smile. Then he held out his treat bag, and in a timid voice, said, "Trick or treat!" She dropped candy into the bag while his face radiated with anticipation.

His sister brings him home. Later, we're sitting on the front steps. I look into the face of the small child of his younger years. I love him more than my own life. I ask him, "Are you happy?"

"Yes," he says.

I feel, no matter what his disabilities are, as long as he's happy, his quality of life is good. After all, isn't finding happiness what we all strive for in our lives?

Car Trouble

Today is respite day. I'm dressing to leave for the day, and Acy demands, "Take me to the hospital. My bowels haven't move all day."

"I'm trying to get ready for my own doctor's appointment."

He starts pacing the floor. "I need to go to the hospital."

"We'll go as soon as I get back."

"No, I want to go now!"

I lose my cool. "Now you look here! This is my day to see the doctor. I need my prescriptions. If I don't see him today, I don't know when I'll get another chance." I point to the bed. "You get over there and lie down, so I can finish dressing!"

He glares at me, then decides to lie down. Within minutes, he's asleep. I'm ready by the time Alice arrives. Acy's awake and has forgotten his little temper tantrum.

It takes an hour and a half to drive to the doctor. When I get there, steam is rising from my car. I smell something burning. I call AAA, and the doctor's receptionist gives them directions. I'm told they will send someone to haul me and my car to the garage. While I wait, I decide to keep my appointment with the cardiologist, and his assistant takes my blood pressure. He makes me tell him about my day. He says he's surprised my blood pressure isn't higher. It's one hundred fifty over eighty. AAA arrives and tows my car to the garage. After an hour, I see that I can't make it home before the caregiver leaves, so I call Bessie. She and Jim agree to stay with Acy until I get home. The mechanic at the garage informs me, when I had my car serviced three days before at a different garage, the cap for the radiator wasn't replaced properly. This caused the antifreeze to steam, spill over, and burn. The thought of this being my day for respite (I don't get another one for two weeks) keeps going through my mind, and I think, *Are we having fun yet?* I can't take the chance of Acy ending up home alone, so I decide there will be no more doctor visits for me. I know everyone says to take care of myself, but the thought of him being left by himself blinds my reasoning.

Pulmonary Aspiration

Acy won't drink his vitamin drink anywhere but on the couch. As he's having his drink, I notice something's wrong. He's not coughing or making any noise, but his mouth is open, and his face is red and looks swollen. The drink has gone down his windpipe. I know what to do, but I'm not sure I know how to do it. I get behind him and put my arms around him the way I have watched it being done. I push a few times, but it seems like forever. Finally, I push, and the drink rolls out of his mouth. He starts breathing and doesn't appear to be aware of what just happened. I tell him that from now on, he's never to drink anywhere but at the table. After this, I will always sit with him when he eats or drinks.

Words Escape Him

I notice a change in Acy's vocabulary. At times, he forgets words. When he wants my attention, he always says, "Hey Faye." This morning, he forgets my name, so he starts yelling. "Heaay! Heaay!"

These soon turns into a sound that is more like chanting. "Heaaaay! Heaaaay!" After some research, I discover there's a name for this. It's called disruptive vocalization.

This goes on for three days. It even happens at night, if he wakes up. He says, "This is the sound of me dying."

He wants to go to the doctor, so I take him. The doctor doesn't help. Acy's vocabulary returns, but all he does is cuss, rant, and rave. Then his vocabulary returns to normal and he settles down.

Once again, Acy loses his vocabulary, and the disruptive vocalization is back in full force. He comes to me and asks if there is anything I can do for him. I tell him no and explain to him that he has Alzheimer's, and this is part of the disease. Up until now, he's denied having Alzheimer's. He says he doesn't want to live this way. He goes to bed, then returns to the living room.

"Why aren't you in bed?" I ask.

"I want to sleep on the couch."

"What's wrong with the bedroom?"

"I'm afraid."

The living room becomes our bedroom.

He asks me not to put him in a nursing home, and I tell him he's already been in one. He can't remember this.

His disruptive vocalization is down to short out-bursts now. He seems to accept his loss of vocabulary. I think he vocalizes when he wants to say something and forgets the words.

I'm sitting at the computer, and trying to ignore his yelling.

"Heaaaaay! Heaaaaaay!"

Then I hear, "I need some earplugs."

I give him a pair of mine.

Later, he sits on the couch with his cat. I sit across the room from him in my rocker. He starts to get rough with the cat, and I yell for him to stop. He jumps off the couch and comes at me, yelling, "Yea, yea, yea, yea, yea."

I think, *Well, I just got cussed out.*

Today, he's angry because he can't get out the front door. He rattles the door and yells, "Let's go. Let's go." Then he opens the window. "Heaaaaaay! Heaaaaaaaaay! Somebody help me."

This continues until we visit Bessie for as long as he wants. Then I bring him home and shave him. This usually puts him to sleep, but not today. He's back at the door again.

"Let's go. Let's go."

He's been in this repetitive mood for two days.

"Heaaaaaaay! Heaaaaaaay!"

I ask, "Why do you do that?"

"I don't know. I can't help it."

I go in search of some aspirin.

Acy's losing his ability to carry on a conversation, but I have a problem I want to share with him. He's watching TV and I'm watching him. I know there can be no productive conversing between us. As I watch him, I say, more to myself than him, "I miss you."

Without hesitation, I hear, "I'm right here."

From that point on, I talk to him as if he understands what I'm saying. Who knows? Maybe he does.

Why Doesn't Mom Call?

Acy thinks his parents are still alive. The common rule used to deal with this delusion is, never mention that the parents have passed away. There isn't any need to take the chance of upsetting him.

We are in the garage and seated in the car. He spots two empty buckets on a shelf. "Save those buckets."

"Why?"

"Dad wants them."

"OK."

He's happy to be doing something for his dad. I see no reason to take this from him. He talks more about his dad than his mom, but he never wonders where Dad is. He thinks his dad's at work. On the other hand, he expects to hear from his mom.

We're in the living room, and he's looking in a dish at some of his trinkets. He's distraught. "I wonder why Mom doesn't call to see how I am."

It bothers me that he thinks his mother is being negligent and uncaring. I move to where he stands and take his hand. I lead him to the couch and tell him we need to talk. I'm not sure how this will play out. I do know that he has always been the type that could deal with the truth better than the unknown. If this ends in grief and crying, I will hold him for as long as he needs. When it's over, he'll know his mother hasn't abandoned him.

I hold his hand and tell him, "Your mom was extremely ill. She had cancer." I pause to give him time to absorb this. "You stayed with her a lot and helped take care of her." I pause again. "You were a great son and did everything you could for her, but she was too sick. She passed away."

"Well, why didn't you tell me?"

I choose my words carefully. "I knew it would hurt you, and I didn't want to cause you pain." I hold my breath.

He sits quietly for a minute, and then asks, "When are we going to eat?"

I breathe again. "Come on. I'll fix you something."

It appears this has bothered me more than him. This kind of confrontation upsets some dementia patients. Others take it in stride. He stops mentioning his mom.

Night Traveling

It's not uncommon for someone with Alzheimer's to want to travel in the middle of the night. Some manage to escape their homes, and become lost in the dark. This situation leads to search teams, and if it's winter, hypothermia or pneumonia can prevail. In a lot of cases, it ends in death.

I wake to find Acy sitting in a chair and holding a paper bag with some of his belongings. I try to be nonchalant. "Whatcha doing?"

Showing no signs of his usual agitated self, he says calmly, "I'm waiting for someone."

"Why?"

"I have to go," he says with the sweetness and innocence of a child.

I know he won't last long in the freezing temperatures outside. Some caregivers secure the exits in their homes and let the patients ramble at will. I decide to try this avenue. The keyed deadbolts on the doors are locked. He checks the door. When it doesn't open, he quietly returns and sits down. The windows are locked, but he has a knack for figuring out locks. I know some people escape this way. The living room window is the only one low enough and big enough for him to escape through. He's afraid of the height from the window to the ground, but I know this could change. I sit in front of this window, and he sits in a chair across from me. He's very patient. It's as if he is waiting for a ride. If only I could kiss him and make it all better. I keep drifting in and out of sleep. He finally tires and beds down on the couch. After a couple of weeks, he passes through this stage with no harm done. Many others are not so lucky. God bless them all.

Christmas

Acy doesn't seem aware that Christmas is at hand. His vocabulary is limited. He can't carry on a conversation, but he can put simple words together. Most of the time, he lies in bed with his eyes closed.

Bessie visits, and we exchange gifts. Acy's eyes remain closed. He says nothing and doesn't respond to her being there. We don't believe he's aware we're in the room. After Bessie and I gossip awhile, we get bored. We feel a little mischievous and start telling dirty jokes. Amid the laughter, we hear, "You dirty girls!"

It turns out, not only is he listening, he catches on to the jokes.

I purchase a small Christmas tree and decorate it. Acy acknowledges the tree and the presents under it, then he seems to lose interest. He doesn't notice when Christmas comes and goes. I can't stand the pain of celebrating the holiday when he isn't alert enough to share it with me. I put the tree and presents away. A few days later, he looks at me with little boy eyes and says, "I missed Christmas."

I could kick myself. How could I do this to him? I could and should have gone through the motions for his sake instead of taking the easy way out for me.

I regret this decision, and I know the guilt will stay with me the rest of my life. I realize this may be his last Christmas.

CHAPTER 7

2010: PART ONE

I Cry

I cry for his daily losses because he can no longer cry for himself. When he wanted to take all our money and spend it, I went to the bank and secured what we had, and I cried for him. When I helped him lose his truck keys and watched for weeks as he hunted for them, I cried for him. When I disposed of his guns, which I hated but he cherished, I cried for him. When I asked the doctor to help me convince the DMV to suspend his driver's license, I cried for him.

As I watch him try to eat, talk, breathe, and go to the bathroom on his own, I cry for him. As he tries to find his way from his new world back to mine, I cry for him. When he says he's glad he has someone he can trust, I think of all I have taken from him, and I cry for him.

I ask myself, *Why should I be the one to lie and be deceitful when he trusts me so much?* Then I realize it's because of this trust that I'm the only one who can do these things, and I cry for me.

I look back over the past, the good and the bad, and then I look to the future, and I cry for us.

Jean

Up until now, Acy's gotten along quite well with his aides. In addition to what the VA furnishes, there are some who are self-employed. Jean's been here a few weeks. She's friendly with me, but problems occur when I'm gone. Acy and she don't make a good match. He becomes agitated when she bathes him. This morning, I walk pass the bathroom door while she's bathing him. I rush into the room. "No! You can't use that to bathe him!"

She's using Clorox wipes to wash his private parts. I put the wipes out of her reach and hope things will get better.

A week later, I leave the house for ten minutes to go next door. When I return, she meets me at the door. I sense something's wrong. She appears shaken and hesitates to tell me something.

"What's wrong?" I ask.

"Acy's upset," she says. "I started to bathe him, and he took my elbow and marched me to the door. He told me he never did let a woman boss him around. I told him where you were and that I had to stay until you returned."

I check on Acy, but whatever happened is long gone from his mind. If he was distraught, I can't tell it now.

I find it odd that the soft drink she brings with her every day is always half full. I decide to check this out. While she bathes Acy, I slip into the kitchen. I remove the bottle from the refrigerator and open it. I pour some in a glass. One sip tells me my suspicions are correct. She's bringing a spiked drink to work. I'm disappointed that I have to let her go.

I'm left with another setback. Once again, Acy refuses to let me bathe him. In time, I hope to gain his confidence back.

The Big Snowstorm
We're in the middle of a brutal snowstorm. Cars and trucks are all along the ditch beside the road. There's no service for the TV or phone. Electrical lines are down, and a blackout covers several states. Trees are lying in the roads and on rooftops. Several trees have fallen around our home.

One is close to the garage, so I bundle up and step out the door to investigate. As I check for damage, the chill cuts through my clothes, and I lower my head to keep the sting of the wind from my eyes. The snow is above my knees, and it impedes my progress. The wind uprooted the tree, and it lies about a foot from the garage.

I return to the house and build a fire in the wood stove. I gather my pots and pans and carry them over to the stove. Before long, the smell of breakfast fills the air. Bellies are full, and the house is warm. The temperature rises in the fridge. I load the food into a Styrofoam container and bury it in the snow by the back door.

There's no running water, but I make do with the bottled water I have on hand. We use the water to drink, cook, and wash dishes. I melt snow to flush the commode.

I wake this morning to a sheet of snow blocking the view outside my window. I open the door to the front porch and see a four-foot wall of snow. I realize it slid from the roof during the night. It runs the length of the house. I check behind the house, and I'm faced with the same fiasco.

I investigate further and discover heavy snow on the metal roof. It eases down the roof and hangs from the gutters.

I go downstairs to find a shovel in the garage. From inside the house, I open the windows, and push the snow off the gutters. I can't reach all of it, so I pray the remaining snow doesn't rip the gutters from the house.

This continues each day. My prayers are answered. The gutters ride the storm out, but they are loose and need to be reinforced.

To my surprise, Acy is cooperative. This is out of character for him. He listens to all my instructions and tries to follow them. He stays on the couch while I'm outside, and he follows me from room to room when I'm inside. He waits patiently while I fix his meals. He understands we're in an emergency and looks to me for guidance.

It's been ten days since it snowed, and it seems as if each day the warm temperatures cause another disaster. I step outside to clean the steps. An avalanche of ice and snow, that's fallen from the roof, greets me. I don't have time to wait for the salt to melt the snow and ice. I shovel the snow and use a pick to break up the ice.

I move back into the house and make my way to the bathroom. There's no window in the bathroom, only darkness. I step inside the door and cringe. I'm standing in some kind of puddle. I don't want to step back onto the carpet. I move forward, and realize

Acy couldn't find the commode. Pee covers the floor. I wade through the pee and grab a mop, bucket, and a pair of rubber gloves. With rubber gloves on, I mop up the pee, and then dry my feet. When I finish, it dawns on me that I have no water to clean the floor, mop, or my feet.

I walk to Jim and Bessie's, and ask them if they will drive to the store and buy me some bottled water. They return with a truckload. Bessie tells me when the store manager heard about my dilemma, he had the employees load the truck from their warehouse. Angels walk among us.

Two days later, they restore the electrical power, and we have water. Now it's bath time.

I've been busy, and neglected the driveway. Over the past week, the snow and ice have fallen from the roof and accumulated on the drive. The ice is packed a foot deep, and it's two feet down the drive. It runs the width of the drive.

I shovel the snow first. Jim sees me and comes over to lend a hand. In two hours, the drive is clear of snow, and we tackle the ice. We peck away at the ice with picks and remove it piece by piece.

Acy and I are finally free to resume our travels. The first stop is Wendy's for a Frosty.

Myrtle

Today is Myrtle's first day, and I want to try a new approach to the bathing. I do the bathing and show

Myrtle the way Acy wants to be bathed. That goes well.

The next time, I stay with them and let her do the bathing while I talk her through it.

She informs me, "I studied 'the book,' and I know how to bathe him."

She demonstrates. She runs the washcloth slowly up and down his back. She tells me this will take longer, but he will enjoy it more.

I laugh to myself. *Sure, honey. Give it a try.*

I have no idea what book she studied, but I'm sure Acy's about to educate her. I leave the room and walk down the hall.

With panic in his voice, I hear Acy yell, "I'm getting the hell out of here!"

I step back in the bathroom and talk to him. "Acy honey, she's new. She doesn't know any better. Let's see if we can teach her how to bathe you."

He isn't completely convinced, but I eventually talk him into giving her another chance. I tell her, "His name's not in your book. He has a book of his own."

Then I talk her through the bath without any problems.

"He's just used to the way you do it," she says.

I correct her. "No, he showed me how he wanted it done, and I do it that way. He can't accommodate your book. You need to work at his level and not from your book."

The rest of the day passes, and she performs her duties without incident.

Myrtle returns later in the week. She decides she used the wrong approach to bathe Acy. She explains that she talked to a friend who's a nurse. The nurse told her dementia patients are to be bathed as quickly as possible.

The damage is done. Acy no longer trusts her and becomes agitated at bath time. I'm tired of undoing the damage untrained aides create. It takes too long to gain back his trust. I bathe him while she reads the paper. I will be bathing him from now on. I see no reason to add to his confusion and upset him. When he's upset, he makes it hard for the rest of us.

The Fall

Acy finishes his breakfast and stands up. He immediately hits the floor, and my heart does too. There's just the two of us, and I'm not sure how to help him. I'm standing over him. "Acy honey, there's no way I can lift you up from the floor." I pull a footstool over to the chair. "Let's try to get you on this footstool."

I place my arms around him and lift upward, and he uses his arms to boost himself onto the footstool. From there, he lifts himself onto the chair.

I roll his wheelchair over to where he's seated. I lift Acy, and his legs are strong enough to hold him up while I guide him into the wheelchair. I guess all that Walmart walking has paid off. He already knows how to maneuver the wheelchair. He learned by watching the people in wheelchairs at the nursing home. His ability to learn always amazes me.

The two of us, and the wheelchair crowd the bathroom. In order to bathe him, he sits in the hall outside the bathroom door, and I bathe him from there. I prepare his folding commode chair in case we need it. I call the VA hospital and put in a request for a bed and a sling lift.

With a little guidance, he easily slips from his wheelchair to the couch. After he sinks into the cushions, he can't help with the move back to the wheelchair. I'm faced with moving him by myself. I know I should try to move him slowly so he isn't startled. I also know I don't have the strength to hold him very long. I do it the quickest way I know. I put my arms around him, lift, and swing him around to the chair in one motion. He's startled, and he yells, but he's in the chair. He makes more of an effort to help himself now, and in two days, he's back on his feet. I put the commode chair away.

I call the hospital to cancel the lift, but I'm told they will send it anyway. That way, we'll be prepared should he fall again. They give me a delivery date for the bed and lift.

While waiting, I push the couch to the other side of the room. I see this as my chance to do some major cleaning. Jim stops by and offers his help. On the side of the room where the bed will sit, we wash the ceiling, walls, and floor. I'm afraid my housecleaning has suffered these past couple of years.

Delivery day is here. They arrive with the bed, and as it's being put together, Acy's excitement grows. When they're finished, he can't wait to lie down. He tells them he had one like it when he was in the army.

They deliver the lift and show me how to use it. It sits at the end of the hall unused.

A Setback

Acy isn't talking, and he's having swallowing problems. For now, his diet consists of Ensure, chocolate milk, and Frostys. His loss of words and swallowing seem to go hand in hand. *Will he snap out of it again?* Only time will tell. I know what the future holds for him, but not in what order. He walks and uses the bathroom, but has trouble finding it.

His spitting has gotten worse, so I put a trash can by his bed. When he spits, some makes its way into the can, and the rest is on the bed, floor, and his table. I have some extra pieces of vinyl flooring, and I put this along the front of the bed where the trash can sits. Each day, the liner in the can is changed, the vinyl and table are washed, and his sheets are changed. I don't breathe while cleaning the can. The odor nauseates me. When Myrtle is here, she helps with everything but the trash can. I can't bring myself to ask her.

Acy's problem, with leaving his spit cup in the car when we go out, is now a common occurrence. I try to keep a supply of spit cups in the car. Still, Acy repeatedly enters the store without one. I make sure he has a cup when I unbuckle his seat belt, but at some point, he sets his cup down as he exits the car. I'm becoming amazingly fast at racing to the aisle where the cups are, while encouraging him not to spit. I continue to break the rules by opening the pack and giving him one, but I pay for them when I check out.

We find our way to the car, and I help him into his seat. As I sit down in the car, he throws his cup out the car window and into the parking lot. I get out of the car and retrieve the cup. Sometimes it rolls under the car, and I have to move the car first. I'm so tired I can hardly walk. I think it's more due to the stress of watching as he slowly disappears before my eyes. When we travel, even with his cup, there is spit on the windshield, the dashboard, and the door on the passenger's side.

Obsession: Ensure & Refrigerator

Acy goes to the refrigerator and stands with the door open, and I step out of the room. When I return, something liquid is running across the floor. I trace it to the trash can. I realize he took an Ensure from the refrigerator, opened it, and threw it in the trash.

He's back at the fridge. He pulls an Ensure from the shelf and drinks it. He keeps going back until he throws up. Then he returns and starts over again.

I take the Ensure from his hand. "Acy honey, you ought to wait awhile to drink any more. You've had so much it's making you sick."

He snatches the Ensure from my hand. "It's my body. I'll do what I want."

He shoves me across the floor and continues raiding the refrigerator. He can't remember he's already eaten.

Acy is now obsessed with the Ensure and the refrigerator. I have to do something. If he continues to drink until he throws up, he's going to hurt himself, and I'm not sure I'm altogether safe. I buy a chain and wrap it around the handles on the doors of our side-by-side fridge. I secure the chain with a lock.

He's furious. He pulls on the handles until he chips the paint on the doors. His voice booms, "Why are you doing this to me? Why do you want to starve me? Don't you care? I wouldn't do this to you."

He can't help it. It's Alzheimer's.

I open the fridge, and a fight ensues. He's pushing and shoving. He's trying to move me out of the way so he can get to the Ensure in the fridge.

Determination anchors my feet to the floor. I gather everything I think I'll need for the next few hours, and place it in a cooler.

When Myrtle's here, I put everything they will need in the cooler, and then chain the door. This way, she can tell him she can't open it either, and he won't blame her.

Acy no longer drinks his Ensure from the bottle. He can only drink through a straw. The problem is, once he starts sucking through the straw, he can't stop until it's all gone. I sit with him and slow him down by removing the straw from his mouth. I tell him to breathe. This is our new normal.

At his next doctor's appointment, the doctor asks, "How's your appetite?"

"Not very good," Acy answers.

The doctor turns to me.

"He's drinking Ensure," I say.

The doctor writes something in his notes. "How much?"

"Ten bottles a day," I say.

The doctor drops his pencil and rolls his eyes. I don't mention the Frostys.

It's time to weigh in. Acy's gained thirty pounds.

Car Shopping

When I take Acy out for his daily ride, he has trouble getting out of the car. He pulls and I tug until

I lift him from the seat. The car's become an insufficient ride for us. I'm looking for something with more cargo space in case he needs his wheelchair or walker. I decide it's time to shop for transportation. I can't find anyone to leave Acy with, so I take him with me. We stop at Cole Motors to see what they have in stock. Acy doesn't understand what's happening. I check out a number of vehicles before I decide on an SUV. I use my car as a trade-in. Acy has no opinion whatsoever. He has no idea what's happening. Even though he's with me, I'm alone. Like a parrot, he keeps repeating, "Let's go. Let's go."

While doing the paperwork, he keeps slipping out the door, and I must go after him. When it's time to transfer our belongings, I put Acy in the SUV first. I carry a load from the trunk of the car to the SUV, and he's gone. The salesman tells me Acy's in the car. I leave him there until I finish. The salesman helps watch after him and take care of him so I can go to the bathroom. When we're ready to leave, the salesman hugs me. If Acy's aware of what transpired, he doesn't show it.

We're almost home. Acy recognizes when we're getting close to home. As we approach the last curve before we reach home, he says, "You need to slow down." I've gotten so used to this, that when I go out by myself and return, I drive by the house.

After three days, Acy can recognize the SUV in the parking lot. I help him into his seat and move toward the cargo area. I raise the cargo door, turn, and there he stands. He refuses to sit in the SUV. He wants to know what I'm doing. He has no problem climbing in and out. He watches me with fascination as I raise the door and load the packages. The SUV is a big hit.

The Social Scene
Walmart is Acy's social center. When we're there, he has the chance to see his old buddies. He still knows most of them. He's very cordial and hasn't forgotten his manners. He's always been a quiet person, so all he has to do is smile and nod in agreement, and his friends can't believe he's sick. Some are more sensitive and seem puzzled by his confusion. Others leave with tears in their eyes.

Today, while I'm at Walmart, I spot Myrtle and approach her. She tells me that if she didn't know Acy was in the later stages of Alzheimer's, she would never suspect he's sick. Since she helps take care of him, she understands the work that goes into washing, shaving, and dressing him for his daily outing.

Myrtle tells me Acy and I are the talk of Walmart. Everyone says how adorable the elderly couple is, holding hands as they walk through the parking lot. Other friends also mention people talking about the sweet old couple at Walmart, holding hands. If they only knew, the hand-holding is to keep Acy from getting lost.

New Stage

Acy enters a new stage. He's checking everything out. He stands in front of the TV and keeps turning it on and off. I'm afraid he will pull it over on himself, so I unplug the TV.

He's now playing with the controls on the air conditioner. I try to stop him, but he grabs my arms. I tell him if he harms me, I'll call the police. He decides to go take a nap. I set a screen from a storm door in front of the air conditioner and tie it so he can't move it.

He wakes from his nap. He can't remember how to turn the light on. He takes the lightbulbs out of the lights and claims they're blown. He begins putting his fingers in the sockets. I unplug the lights.

I read somewhere to hide everything from them that has a potential for danger. If only I could figure out how to hide the lights, TV, refrigerator, and air conditioner.

His Temper Tantrum

Acy has been cussing at me and threatening me for some time. Until now, he's managed to do this when we're alone. Today, he's standing by his bed, leaning on a table. I tell him, "Don't lean on the table. It won't hold your weight, and you could fall and get hurt."

Without missing a beat, his face distorts with anger. "Damn you! I'm going to beat the hell out of you!"

He launches across the room. To his surprise, the aide is watching from the hall. He forgot she was there.

I say with more courage than I feel, "You need to go back before you get in trouble."

He retreats and lies down. *He can't help it. It's Alzheimer's.*

After a year of this kind of behavior, this is the first time he's done it in front of someone. The aide comments, "You did a good job backing him down."

"Thank goodness he didn't call my bluff."

Before the aide leaves, she says, "I'll see you tomorrow."

I reply, "If Acy didn't scare you off."

"You don't need to worry about that."

Myrtle finds a lady to take care of.

On Our Own Again

Things are moving smoothly without the extra help. We make our trip to Walmart and Wendy's every day. Sometimes we make this trip twice a day.

Acy is happy, and if he's happy, then I'm happy. Bessie comes over and stays with him when I need to go out by myself. Acy has formed unique bonds with us. He treats me like I'm his mother and she's his favorite aunt.

Since Bessie works during the day, I take Acy with me when I go to the bank. I tell him I need money to pay for his Frosty. He enters the bank, sits down, and waits for me. He behaves himself. He knows the reward will be a Frosty.

The staff at Wendy's is always good to him. They come over to our table to visit with him. They keep their eyes on him while I'm in line. The staff alerts me when Acy leaves the table. We often find him going to the empty tables and gathering the unused napkins. He loves these napkins because they're yellow. I always give him some before we leave. When we leave, if the staff isn't busy, they wave to him, and he waves back. He waves like a two-year-old. Sometimes I feel as if he has given me the child I never had.

Once a week, we take a two-hour drive. Today, we stop at Arby's. After we order, we're told there aren't any napkins. Acy says, "That's OK."

He pulls out his Wendy's napkins. Here we sit in the middle of Arby's, with Wendy's napkins on the table. The yellow napkins with red writing scream Wendy's.

On the way home, we stop to visit Bessie. To show his affection for her, he offers her his Wendy's napkins. She lays them on the table. After a few minutes of her showing no sign of interest in the napkins, he scoops them up. "If you don't want these..."

Before he can finish, Bessie grabs them. "No, no. I want them. They sure are pretty." She smooths them out in her lap.

Acy beams with pride and says, "They're valuable." She holds them in her lap for the rest of the visit.

Two days later, I need to talk to Bessie, and Acy tags along. We're standing by the counter in the kitchen. Out of the corner of my eye, I see him reach for something on the counter. Bessie grins. I look over my shoulder long enough to see Acy pick up the Wendy's napkins and put them in his pocket. We laugh and continue our conversation. He goes home with the napkins.

A few days later, Acy becomes aggressive during another visit at Wendy's. Someone is sitting at the booth where we always sit. I show him to another table. I tell him, "Sit in this chair so we can see each other from the checkout line."

He sits for about a second, than moves to a chair where his back is to the checkout line. I know if he can't see me, he'll walk out the door and roam the parking lot to look for me.

"Acy, you need to sit here so we can see each other," I say. I point at the first chair.

I help him up, and we start back to the first chair. He stops and pushes me. Everyone watches us. I point at the door, and in a firm voice, I say, "If you don't sit down, I'm walking out that door, getting in the SUV, and leaving here."

He gives in and sits down.

I order his Frosty and set it on the table. While we eat, I look up from my chili in time to see him spit a mouthful of Frosty back into his cup. Before I can react, he scoops the spit up with his spoon and puts it back in his mouth.

I'm nauseated. My meal comes to an end. I become distraught watching him try to eat. It bothers me to see how far he's fallen.

After we return home, I begin to itch. I check to see what's wrong, and I'm breaking out in hives. They're spreading at an alarming rate. I call Jim, and he goes to the pharmacy for antihistamines. I take them, and he stays with us awhile. The antihistamines are working. I've been told hives are caused by stress. I fear I'm close to having a nervous breakdown.

His disruptive vocalization is worse. He does this off and on all day, especially when he can't get out the door and I ignore him as he chants, "Let's go. Let's go." I now take him out twice a day, but he forgets.

Tonight he wakes up around 2:00 a.m., and yells, "Heaaaaaaaay. Heaaaaaay" until he falls asleep. This is becoming an every night thing. I try putting a CD in the CD player and turning it on. His becomes distracted and listens to the music. This doesn't work during the day. He finds the player and pushes buttons until he turns it off.

I can't sleep with the CD player on. When I try to nap in the day, he sees my eyes closed and claps his hands until I open them. *He can't help it. It's Alzheimer's.* I think, *Oh well. Who needs sleep anyway?*

My Temper Tantrum

Acy's lying in bed, and becomes agitated. For two years, he has been threatening to whip my ass. After months of fighting me and putting bruises on my arms, once more he tells me, "I'm going to whip your ass!"

My stress is through the roof. *If whipping my ass is what you want to do, then let's get it over with.* I leap across the floor to his bed. I start shaking my fists at him and tell him, "Get up off that bed and give it your best shot."

It surprises him and causes him to forget what he said. He looks at me as if he's wondering how he ended up with the crazy woman. He makes no move to get off the bed, and I feel foolish. *I can't help it. It's Alzheimer's.*

It seems his hostility is only aimed at me. I think about calling the VA and saying I can't take this anymore. This is the most thankless job I know. Never mind that Acy can no longer find the bathroom and goes where it's convenient for him. Never mind he can't shave, dress, or wash himself. Never mind that I clean his glasses, wipe his rump, clean pee from the bathroom floor, and clean the floor and table where he spits. What I hate is, when he tries to boss me around and ridicules me. He knows very few words, so this doesn't bode well for him. I hate, that I am glad for this. When he tries to talk, I know it's nothing I want to hear. I'm angry because for all I do, this is all I get in return.

Feeling Guilty

I feel guilty for the lies I tell. I feel guilty for some of the choices I make. I feel guilty for being impatient at times and scolding him when I know he can't help the things he does. Other caregivers tell me I shouldn't feel guilty. Then I notice these same caregivers have their own feelings of guilt for one reason or another. We know we shouldn't, but we do anyway.

I've given this some thought. I think guilt is normal, and makes us better caregivers. It shows we care for and love our spouses and would never intentionally hurt them. Isn't being sorry for things we say or do better than not caring at all? Isn't it better than enjoying watching our loved ones suffer while in our care?

The way I see it, I have three options for the things I say or do. I can enjoy any suffering my mistakes inflict, I can stop caring at all, or I can feel guilty. I've decided I'd rather feel guilty.

I've apologized more than once to Acy for turning mean-spirited. He seems to understand, so I see no reason to continue beating myself up for this. It shows I love and care enough to do the very best I can. After all, I'm sure the things I feel guilty about are small compared to all the selfless acts I perform.

The next time I feel guilty, I will remember it comes from love, and it's better than not caring at all. Acy and I have been married many years. Long ago, he accepted that I wasn't perfect, and he made the choice to forgive and love me anyway. I'm sure he would want me to forgive myself.

The Door

Acy is on another rampage to get out the front door and into the street. "Let's go. Let's go."

I have the deadbolt locked, and wear the key around my neck. He threatens me, so I remove the key and hide it. That way, I won't get choked. The back door is unlocked, but he sees the road from the front. He's kicking the door. He wants to kick it down.

"Acy, you shouldn't do that. You almost fell. If you fall, I won't be able to pick you up."

"That's all right. I'll kick it again!" he says.

Boom. The sound shatters my nerves.

I check the door, and he's loosened the door-knob. While I'm checking this, he comes at me with some magazines he's rolled into a tight bundle. I swing and hit his arm, and magazines scatter across the room. He grabs my arms and leaves bruises on them. I struggle free, but he comes at me again. I grab his arms, pin them to his sides, and spin him around. He becomes confused, and I tell him to sit on the couch. He backs off and sits on the couch.

I call the hardware store to see if they have a ther-mometer cover. They do, so we drive to the store and buy the cover. I install it over the doorknob. Now he kicks the cover. The noise is so loud the neighbors can hear him. He turns to me. "Let me out of here! I'm going to catch a bus!"

There are no buses.

I tell him, "Let me help you pack."

He's hurt. "You're trying to throw me out. Please don't leave me." Then he informs me, "We need to go. We're going to get locked up in here."

I lead him to his bed. "Do you see this? This is your bed. You live here. Why don't you lie down and take a load off?"

He lies down, and soon he's asleep.

A couple of days later, I'm listening to the door being mutilated. I'm standing in front of the kitchen stove cooking. Without warning, he's behind me. He swings me around and pins me against the stove. "Give me that key!"

I don't have time to hide it. He puts his fist in my face.

"Don't do that! The police will put you in jail."

He's focused on the key. "I don't care! I want that key."

There's no way I can free myself, so I reluctantly give him the key. I need to save myself before I can save him. He heads for the door. By the time I turn the stove off and put my shoes on, he's across the road. His cousin sees him and stops to talk to him. I cross the road to find he has forgotten the incident.

His cousin asks, "How old are you?"

He ponders this for a minute. He turns to me. "How old am I?"

"You'll be seventy next week."

Without hesitation, he asks his cousin, "Are you coming to the party?"

I wasn't aware there was a party. He'd always thought such things were childish.

He returns home with a smile on his face. *He can't help it. It's Alzheimer's.*

CHAPTER 8

2010: PART TWO

Are We Married? Part Two

Acy's at the door doing his thing. He gives the door a kick that would put a mule to shame. His disruptive vocalization is in full swing. I need a distraction, so I fire up the computer. Acy's never cared for the computer. He thinks I should spend all my time catering to him. He spots me from the other room and stomps toward me. He shakes his finger at the computer. "You tell your boss..."

I stop him midsentence. Joking, I say, "You're my boss."

He stops and studies my face. *Oh, crab. Thirty-five years of learning to compromise just went down the drain.* I now have someone with the mind of a two-year-old trying to control my every move.

To stop him from kicking the door today, we visit Bessie. After five minutes, he says, "Let's go."

"We'll go in a minute. Let Bessie finish talking."

He stomps around the living room, then moves toward the door. "I'll just get me another one."

Another what? I wonder.

We return home, but his comment keeps running through my mind. Finally, it dawns on me. He's treating me the way he did when we were first married, when he thought he should be the boss.

I ask, "Are we married?"

He says with authority in his voice, "Yes!"

Life was so much easier when he didn't know we were married. At least he didn't think he owned me.

Pee and Poop Patrol

Acy's having trouble controlling his bladder when we go out. I have to be ready at a moment's notice to get him to a bathroom. We're in Walmart when I see him reach for the zipper of his pants. We're in the middle of the store, and I panic. I can't remember the layout of the store. I'm short, and the shelves are mountains. All I can see is the ceiling. I notice the tops of the walls, so I head toward one. Bathrooms are always along a wall. He keeps trying to unzip his pants. I keep grabbing his hand. I hope no one thinks he's being molested. As we cross the floor, I have no idea where we are, but I keep telling him we're almost there. I spot the bathroom and quickly grab his hand. We rush toward it. A disaster is avoided. I don't know how much longer I can keep up this pace. My goal is to keep him walking until the end. That and to keep him going to the bathroom on his own.

We follow down the path Alzheimer's dictates. We know we won't win this war, but we've won another battle.

I find a bathroom routine that works at home, for now. Acy has trouble hitting the commode when he pees. I take pads the VA gave me and cut them in half. I cut them so they fit around the commode. They don't catch all the pee, but they do catch most of it.

I notice when Acy wipes after pooping, he's not quite getting the job done. I want to figure out a way to help him and still keep his ego intact.

The next time he goes to poop, I follow. I get my office chair, and sit in the hall with the bathroom door open. I tell him, "I hope you don't mind. I sure am lonesome, and I could use some company."

He's too busy to answer. He's ready to clean, and I notice he's having a bit of a problem.

I ask, "You need some help with that?"

He says, "OK." His eyes say, "I can use all the help I can get."

I resolve to put his fear of getting poop on himself and his clothes to good use. I want to impose good bathing habits. I tell him, "I need to bathe you to get all the poop off."

He moves to the sink.

I've found a way to bathe him without a fight, or so I think. Some days, he becomes suspicious.

"Let me see that washcloth," he says.

I ad-lib. "Oh, I've already washed you. Now I'm rinsing."

A few weeks go by. Today, the light goes out in the bathroom, and I catch Acy standing in the doorway. He's spraying pee across the bathroom floor. I turn another light on, and he decides to walk through the pee to get to the mop. I stop him, and a scuffle ensues. He points to the floor. "Look! Look!"

"I know! I know! I'm going to take care of it."

I take him by the hand, and lead him to the couch. I grab my rubber gloves, and use paper towels to clear a path to the light. I retrieve a bulb from the cupboard and finish the job.

Several nights pass. Acy walks in the living room and approaches me. He opens the fly of his pajamas and says, "Look at this."

I see he's concerned about something. I take him in the bathroom to see what's wrong. I detect a foul odor, so I check his pajamas. He's messed on himself, and it's thin. I tell him, "Don't move. I'm going to slip your pajamas down."

I ease the pajamas downward.

He bends over. "Yikes!"

It splatters all over the floor, toilet, tub, litter box, wall, and my legs. There's no jump in my blood pressure. Instead, I'm in a state of shock. Before I can think, he steps back in it.

I tell him several times to step forward. I lean over, and I use my hand to push his foot forward. He doesn't like me pushing him, and he's a bit miffed. He pushes back, and we both land in poop. *He can't help it. It's Alzheimer's.*

"If we're ever going to get out of this poop, you'll have to do what I say," I tell him.

After a struggle, we find ourselves upright and standing on the floor. I wash my hands and put on my rubber gloves. I clean the toilet seat off, and wash his bottom. He sits down on the toilet. I clean him and then the middle of the floor. I wash my feet and fetch clean clothes to dress him. I lead him to the couch, and turn on the TV.

I return to the bathroom. The poop has dried on the walls, tub, litter boxes, and my legs. This is a job for the scrub brush. I shower and dump our clothes in the washing machine with a half a bottle of Lysol. It dawns on me I forgot to put his socks on him.

I'm too traumatized to sleep, and too tired to stay awake. I doze off and on through the night. My new motto is, "Give me my rubber gloves, and I can do anything."

A few days pass. We survived the poop-capades. We are ready for our journey to Wendy's. Afterward, we stop at the store to buy a few groceries. We load our cart, and we're in the checkout line. I place the food on the counter, and the cashier is ringing up the order. I'm paying for our purchases when, out of the corner of my eye and to my right, I notice a sudden movement. I glance toward the movement in time to see Acy run from the building. I run after him. By the time I'm outside, he's standing at the SUV. He yells, "Hurry! Hurry!"

I unlock his door and see to it he's buckled in his seat. I race back to the store to retrieve the groceries. I'm worried about what caused his sudden exit. I'm confused and somewhat anxious by the time I return to the SUV. I ease into my seat and calmly ask, "Are you OK?"

"Yes."

"What happened back there?"

He fidgets in his seat. With panic in his voice, he yells, "Let's go! Let's go!"

With a sympathetic voice, I ask, "Can you tell me why you ran from the store?"

He looks at me, and his eyes plead for understanding. "I pissed on myself."

He needs reassurance to help calm him down. "It's OK, baby. No one noticed." His face softens, and his muscles unclench. "You're wearing thick underwear. It caught all the pee. You didn't get your clothes dirty."

His body relaxes, as he leans back in his seat.

We arrive home, and I lead him to the bathroom and help him clean up.

Last Trip to Walmart

We're off to Walmart to get a flu shot. Acy stands behind me in the line. He tries to spit in the cup, but the spit sprays through the air. He's spitting on me. Like everyone else I know, I don't enjoy being spit on. Every time he spits on me, I want to scream. *He can't help it. It's Alzheimer's.*

I'm losing patience. Then I realize it could be worse. He could be spitting on other people. Still, with every spit wad that hits my neck, I cringe. I bow my head. *Lord, please give me the patience and strength to keep my mouth shut.*

A bad day is about to turn worse. He goes out the door while I unload our cart at the checkout line. By the time I get outside, he's halfway across the parking lot. I call to him, but he won't stop. I yell, "Acy, stop! Stop!"

He slows down, and I catch up to him. He turns on me. "If you yell at me again, I'll whip your ass!"

I have an overwhelming urge to get in the SUV and drive until the sound of his threats stop ringing in my ears. *He can't help it. It's Alzheimer's. As hard as this is for me, it's even harder for him.*

I walk him back to the SUV. "Acy honey, I had to yell so you could hear me."

Instead of climbing into the SUV, he tries to open the door of a truck parked beside him. There's a lady in the truck. Thank God she locked the door. As of this moment, he's lost his freedom to walk alone.

I'm Tired

I'm tired of Acy turning off the TV while I'm watching it. I'm tired of him demanding I turn off the computer. I'm tired of his disruptive vocalization. I'm tired of him rattling the doorknob so hard he loosens it and I have to retighten it. I'm tired of him kicking the cover I placed over the doorknob. I'm tired of him kicking it so hard the neighbors complain. I'm tired of him grabbing me and putting his fist in my face. I'm tired of the foul language. I'm tired of being threatened. I'm tired from three years of cleaning spit off everything, including myself. I'm tired of cleaning poop off everything, including myself. I'm so tired that when I enter Walmart alone, the staff takes one look at me and asks if I want to use the motorized cart. I'm so tired that a stranger watching me cross the parking lot tells me I should have parked closer. I'm tired of the handicap spots always being full. I'm so tired I try to give Acy's medicine to his aide. I'm so tired that when I get dressed, I put on two pair of panties. I am SO TIRED.

Cory Dies

It's a sad day around here. One of Acy's cats, Cory, dies. Acy doesn't remember Cory, but he knows this is a somber occasion. I need to bury Cory, but I can't leave Acy alone.

I prepare the cat for burial. I decide to carry the cat, so I ask Acy to help me. I hand him a shovel. He stares at the shovel, and it's clear he has no idea how to grip the handle. It's sad that Cory died. It's also sad that through Acy's lifetime, he's gone from learning to use a shovel to building homes, and now he's returned to his early childhood. He can't figure out how to lift the shovel off the ground. I take his hand, wrap it around the shovel, and show him how to lift it.

We go behind the garage to find a burial spot. I return to the garage to look for something to help dig in the dirt.

I find a mattock, and as I step outside, I see Acy. He's holding the shovel and trying to figure out how to push it into the ground. I realize he wants to help. He doesn't see me, and I want to keep his pride intact, so I wait. After several failed attempts, he stops and lays the shovel down. I approach him, and we bury Cory. We're ready to return home, so I take his hand to guide him.

A few days later, he points toward Cory's bed. "What happened to the cat?"

I tell him, "He passed away."

How much further can he fall? I ache deep inside at the very thought of this.

Sanity Escapes Us

If he isn't kicking the door, he's vocalizing. The only time I get relief is when we go out. He never vocalizes in public.

This morning, I hear his battle cry.

"Let's go. Let's go."

He kicks the door. Boom! Boom! He races to the window. "Heaaaaaaay! Heaaaaaaaay! Somebody help me! Heaaaaaaay! Heaaaaaay!" He seems focused on the vocalization. He continually yells, "Heaaaaaaaaaay!"

He shows no sign of stopping. What do I do? I do what any red-blooded American would do. I cut loose with my rendition of a Carol Burnett Tarzan call. This quietens him down instantly. I believe he thinks I'm crazy.

I give him his medicine. Some time passes, and things are quiet. I go to the door to check on him, and he's sitting by the door in a chair. He's slumped over and asleep.

I feel I am being pulled into this disease with him. The Alzheimer's demon is consuming Acy's brain with its plaques and tangles and is now using Acy to destroy me. *He can't help it. It's Alzheimer's.* I fight for him. I fight for me.

His constant vocalization and begging for help reminds me that I once thought the worst thing to endure would be watching a loved one begging for help at the window of a burning building. I'm no longer sure of this. Watching Acy die bit by bit as days turn into years makes me realize there is a slower, more agonizing death than by fire.

He's reaching the point where his mind can no longer support his vital organs. He seems aware of this as he begs me to help him. He thinks I can do anything. I'm totally helpless as I watch Alzheimer's snuff out his life, much like the smoke from the flames of a fire. I think it would be less painful if it were me.

The days run together. Peace can't be found. His quality of life is poor, and mine's not much better. I know peace can be had for both of us with the pull of a trigger. I make a conscious decision to continue the struggle, knowing I have an option. I know one thing for certain. If I survive, I will never be the same again. *God, give me strength and keep me sane.*

Pneumonia

Acy's having breathing problems while he sleeps. He stops breathing for short periods and then starts again. He makes odd sounds from his throat. I panic and wake him, and he becomes agitated. "What do you think you're doing?"

"There's something wrong. You're not breathing right."

"Well, leave me alone. I'm trying to sleep."

It's hard to sit night after night and do nothing. I roll him on his side, and this seems to help.

I take Acy to Wendy's today. I notice his breathing is heavy as we walk across the parking lot. By the time we're back home, I'm worried. I decide he needs to go to the hospital.

We arrive at the VA hospital and enter the emergency room. He's admitted. A nurse checks his vitals. She asks, "What's your name?"

After some thought, he says, "I don't know."

She points toward me. "Who's this?"

Without hesitation, he says, "My wife."

The nurse is speechless. He's always told them he's not married.

The doctor examines him, and the diagnosis is pneumonia. I talk to the doctor and tell him I have heard pneumonia is part of the last stage. I know a lot of people don't seek treatment for this and choose to let nature take its course. I need to make a decision.

The doctor says, "He can be treated successfully for a long time. Who says he shouldn't be treated?"

I look him straight in the eye and stare him down. In a voice that could pin an Olympic wrestler to the floor, I say, "He does! He wanted to end his life back when he had access to his guns. I stopped him by hiding the guns. I don't think it's fair he be forced to live when nature says it's time to go."

The doctor backs off. Now I'm given space to think. As his power of attorney, I have to make this decision. He can still walk. He wears protective underwear when traveling. He's still active enough to eat out every day. As far as I can tell, he's only been sick one day. I agree to a round of antibiotics. If this works but pneumonia starts repeating, then I will rethink my position.

They move him to his room and start his antibiotics. By the time I get upstairs, they have him in a wheelchair. He's sitting by the nurses' station. There is a lot of traffic in the hall, so I take him to his room, and we visit for a spell. It's time for me to leave, so I push him back to the nurses' station. He sits by the desk with the elevator in sight. I tell them it would be better if they turn him so he can't see me leave. I'm ignored. As I head down the hall, I think, *Oh boy, are you people about to learn a lesson.*

While I wait for the elevator, he panics. He's yelling for me to wait for him. They have a tray slid onto the wheelchair arms so he can't get up, or so they think. He's pulling. He's twisting. They stand around and watch. Acy manages to get his foot in the seat, and he is coming out of the chair. One of the aides rushes to him and stops him from toppling the chair. The CNA exclaims, "He sure is agile!"

Finally they get it. They take him around to the other side and turn him where he can't see me leave.

I'm reminded of an event I witnessed while visiting Acy at the nursing home. The time came for a male visitor to leave his lady friend one afternoon. They were sitting across the room from the front door. He crossed the room and walked out the door. She tried to stand from her wheelchair and fell to the floor. Never taking her eye off the door, she crawled across the floor, pulled herself up by the bars on the wall, and struggled onward toward the door. This is where one of the nursing home aides found her.

I asked Acy, "Would you act like that if I left?"

He answered, "Yeah!"

I learned, never let the dementia patient see you leave, or at least have your story ready.

I return home and stop by Wendy's to update them on Acy's condition. I explain that he's moved into the last stage. "He can't be," they say. "He can still walk."

Someone says, "The lady I know with Alzheimer's has been bedbound for six months."

"Only time will tell," I answer.

It seems there's a lot to be learned about Alzheimer's. The first thing I learned was that no two Alzheimer's patients are alike.

The VA can't find a place for him in any of the dementia units in their network. They're ready to discharge him. His legs have weakened during his hospital stay. Two orderlies dress him, place him in his wheelchair, and help him into the SUV. I'm wondering how I'm going to get him in the house when I arrive home. The social worker says they'll continue to work with me to locate a nursing home for him.

We're home, and I see Jim on the front porch. He crosses the road, and between the two of us, we manage to maneuver Acy into the house and into bed. In a few days, Acy regains strength in his legs.

Nursing Home Number Two

I'm having trouble traveling with Acy. He tries to open the door while the SUV is moving, and he plays with the seat belt.

It reaches the point that I'm not able to take care of outside business, such as shopping and banking. When Acy needs over-the-counter medicine, we wait until Bessie can pick it up after work. The pharmacist brings his prescription medicine to our door. I tell the social worker at the VA hospital, because of his attempts to open the car door, it isn't safe to travel to the hospital for Acy's appointments. She informs me that since he has a 100 percent disability, they will send an ambulance to pick him up.

I can control the locks on the back doors of the SUV, so I try putting him in the back seat. I have no problem helping him in, but his legs are so long and stiff, I'm having trouble maneuvering his legs back out the door. After some manipulation, he's free. It seems the back doors are not as wide as the front.

I decide on a nursing home the VA offers. It's a secure Alzheimer's unit. It's four hours away. I talk to the social worker there, and she answers all my questions to my satisfaction. I hope I'm doing the right thing. I hate to think I have failed him. I expect my visits will be limited. Bessie offers to go with me sometimes. I don't really want to place him, but I'm told he'll do better in the Alzheimer's unit.

We make one last trip to the hospital in the SUV. We're placing him today. The trip is long, and they are going to take him by ambulance. I go upstairs with the social worker to sign some papers. I leave Acy with the CNA who helped him during his hospital stays.

The social worker gets a call from the emergency room. It seems all hell is about to break loose. The ambulance driver has decided to put Acy in the ambulance without waiting for me. Acy begs to differ. He refuses to climb into the ambulance. Now he is being defensive about anyone coming near him. They have called in a VA security guard. I'm worried someone will hurt him if there is a scuffle. Little do they know that he is the least of their worries. If he is hurt in any way, they will have one crazy old woman to deal with. I rush to be by his side. The CNA is there along with a security guard. The two ambulance attendants and several other people are there. They are waiting for a doctor to give him a sedative. I hear an attendant tell the doctor to make it a strong one. I think I could use one now.

I spot him down the hall. Everyone looks anxious. He sees me, and I hold his gaze. As I move closer, I ask, "Are you OK?"

"Yeah."

"Did you know you're going for a ride?"

"No."

"I'm going too."

"Oh."

I continue to hold his gaze. "You need some tests and need to go in the ambulance. I'll follow right behind you."

"OK."

By now, we have a nice size audience. Everyone is quiet. They're watching and listening intently. I hope something is learned. He's tired now and lies down on one of the emergency room beds. He hasn't been admitted to the hospital, so I wait to see if anyone is going to object. I think lying on the bed is the best place for him. Evidently the crowd does too. No one says anything.

He rests for a few minutes and moves back into the hall. He walks toward a door with a "Do Not Enter" sign on it. Nobody moves to stop him. I place myself between him and the door.

"You can't go in there."

He starts to push by me, but my feet are planted firmly on the floor.

"No one is allowed in this room except people who work here."

"Oh."

"Let's go back in this room where we can sit on the bed for a while."

"OK."

As we enter the room, I hear the social worker and CNA commenting about the way I talk to him and how I managed to quieten him down. I hope they carry away something from this that will help further down life's path.

The doctor gives him a shot, and we are on our way to the nursing home. We arrive, and the attendants say Acy kept wanting to get up, but they kept telling him I was following behind them. I'm thankful the doctor chose not to over sedate him.

In the nursing home, I sign papers and make sure Acy is settled in his room. As I leave, I look down the hall. He's all smiles. He's helping push the medicine cart. It never occurs to me this will be the last time I'll ever see him this happy and full of life.

Even though it's Thanksgiving, I stay away to give him time to adjust. I can't stay away any longer. I must see how he's doing. I find him sitting and staring into space. He looks forlorn. It depresses me to see him like this. *Will he know me?*

He sees me. "How did you find me?"

"It wasn't easy."

It dawns on me he's been waiting and wondering if he'll ever see me again.

Things are not going well here. He's in a locked down area, and he's been trying to kick in the door. A staff member tells me he charges the door and hits it with his shoulder.

In my care, he was living on Ensure. They insist he eat pureed food. I try to explain to them he can no longer eat pureed food. I tell them I've been giving him his nourishment by straw for a year. I also explain that during his hospital stays, the VA hospital gives him his nourishment by straw.

Someone mentions that Ensure costs too much. I remind them there are equivalent drinks at lower prices. Another person informs me they go by 'the book'. I remember 'the book' and the problems Myrtle had with 'the book'. *Damn 'the book'! I've never seen it, but I'm still betting his name's not in it.* 'The book' is only written for the average patient. I believe each person should be cared for according to their own unique needs.

He's losing weight and has become constipated for the first time in years. They're giving him enemas, and now his hemorrhoids are bleeding. They call and inform me they're sending him to a civilian hospital.

I make the four hour drive to the hospital. I find Acy asleep. I go to the desk and ask to see the doctor. I wait the rest of the day, all night, and into the next day. No one bothers to talk to me. Acy isn't awake at any point during my visit. One of the hospital staff tells me he isn't eating. I don't think I could either if I were drugged to the point of not knowing the food's sitting there.

I make the four hour trip back home so I can catch up on my sleep. I know the time is close at hand for me to make a decision.

I weigh my pros and cons. The pros for me are, that it's in my favor to continue the fight. I'll still have my husband and my income. Even though he's not with me, I can still visit him. The cons are, that without him, I'll be a widow with very little income.

On the other hand, I know he's counting on me to carry out his wishes. He believes if there's no hope of survival, a person should be allowed to die with dignity. The decision is mine to make and mine to live with. This is on my mind when the phone rings.

The doctor's finally decided to talk to me. He says Acy's in good health physically, but since he isn't eating, they want to put in a feeding tube, and they want to do a colonoscopy because of the bleeding. I have power of attorney, and they need my signature. Without hesitation, I make the only decision I ever really had. I tell them there's to be no treatment and no tests that lead to treatment. The only treatment he's to receive is for comfort.

The doctor says that since that's the case he's going to put it in Acy's records that no one is to feed him. I tell him if they can't feed Acy return him immediately to the nursing home. He agrees.

I leave home and make good time on the road. I arrive at the nursing home, and I'm told they have instructed the hospital to not bring him back. They say I can find him there.

The hospital is not in the same town as the nursing home. I know they won't release Acy this late. I make the long journey back home. I intend to start early the next morning to find my husband.

The next morning, I'm getting ready to leave, and the social worker from the VA hospital calls to tell me the nursing home has informed her of the circumstances. She tells me not to worry. She'll contact the civilian hospital where he's a patient and send an ambulance to bring him home. Finally, someone who cares.

She asks me about hospice. Since I have already talked to them, I'm familiar with their procedures. I tell the social worker that according to the hospice worker I talked to, it will take two weeks to approve someone for hospice. Judging by what the doctor said, I feel it's too late. We end our conversation, and within the hour, she calls back.

She informs me Acy will soon be on his way home. He should arrive sometime tonight. She says that when he gets there, no matter how late, hospice will be there to sign him up.

Hospice

He's at home now, and he's happy. His drugs are wearing off.

"I missed you," he says.

"I missed you too, baby." I lean in close to him. I hold him in my arms, give him a kiss and say, "I love you."

He whispers, "I love you too."

Even though it's late at night, the representative from hospice arrives and qualifies him for hospice.

I tell the representative that one of her coworkers informed me if a patient is mobile enough to walk to the car, that patient is disqualified for hospice. I tell her if he wants to go to Wendy's and is able, I will take him. She believes that is wishful thinking. *We'll see about that.* She agrees and hospice will take effect immediately. A nurse will visit twice a week to check his vitals and manage his medicine. There will also be an aide to bathe him.

A few days later, Madge from hospice, stops by to get acquainted. As we talk, she suggests I compile my experiences as a caregiver for a dementia patient. It's something to think about.

Acy declined during his nursing home stay. He's in protective underwear, but he moves them out of his way and pees through the leg and onto the carpet. He was having trouble finding the bathroom, but doesn't bother to look now. He holds his head lower, and I have to force him to look up. His speech is all but gone. He knows only a few words. He shows no aggression. There's no more disruptive vocalization. He now walks with a shuffle. I've taken him off his medicine to see if it helps. If he becomes aggressive again, I will give him his medicine. He's officially been declared to be in in the last stage of this disease.

The Last Hurrah
Acy's alert today, and he's ready to go. He drinks Ensure through a straw with my assistance. He wants

a Frosty, and I agree. He walks to the car on his own two feet, and I drive him to Wendy's. It's cold, so I use the drive-through. I give our order while the person ahead of us receives theirs. He's bouncing in his seat. He points at the car ahead of us. "Look! Look!"

We watch as the cashier hands the bags of food to someone in the car.

The car pulls away, and Acy says, "That made me hungry."

We park, and I hand him his Frosty. He eats half of it.

I know I made the right decision. A thousand days spent lingering in a hospital bed, knocked out by drugs, and being kept alive with a feeding tube can't compare to these few minutes of happiness.

We travel to Wendy's five more days to eat Frostys. Acy eats less each day.

Today, while we're at Wendy's, he eats two or three spoonfuls of his Frosty. This is his last trip. I prepare for the end of our journey.

CHAPTER 9

THE STRUGGLE

December 13

I need to move Acy's bed. One side runs along the wall, and it's inconvenient, if not downright impossible, to care for him. Thank goodness for wheels. In short order, I rearrange the living room. The head is now against the wall. That leaves the sides and end open. This way, it'll be easier to help him from both sides.

Acy doesn't seem to care for this new arrangement. He refuses to stay in the bed, and he lies on the couch. He wanders into the bathroom, and I hustle over to the couch. I flip it over and onto the floor. I look up to see him entering the living room. I rush to him and help him to bed. He falls asleep, and I tend to the dishes in the kitchen. I return to find him standing at the couch. I watch as he pulls and tugs on the couch to no avail, then collapses into his wheelchair.

December 14
Peace and quiet prevail this morning. Then Acy tells me, "I'm dying."

His pain surges through my body, and I have trouble breathing. "What makes you think that?"

He says, "I'm sorry."

"Why would you be sorry? You haven't done anything wrong."

He falls silent, and takes a nap.

He wakes from his nap. It's noon, and I ask him, "Do you want something to eat?"

"Yeah."

He no longer drinks Ensure. I don't have a Frosty, so I feed him some ice cream, but he spits it out. Later, I give him ginger ale, but he can't keep it down.

Some say maybe he'll get better, but he's already made so many comebacks. I feel this time is different. I've propped him up for the past two years, but I don't see it happening any longer. I know how to fight for life. I don't know how to give in to death. I sit with him and wonder how I'll be able to help him through to the end. Despair embraces me.

December 15

The nurse visits, and we discuss his decline. She mentions his options and asks, "What about a feeding tube?"

I've done my homework. I tell her, "I searched the Internet. Statistics show twenty to thirty percent die within a month after receiving a feeding tube. There are skin infections to deal with, and some are still vulnerable to aspiration pneumonia. And a lot of them pull on the tube, so they have to be sedated or have their arms tied," I say. "I wouldn't treat a dog that way, just to keep it alive. I don't see any comfort in that."

As she checks his vitals, she agrees. She tells me his vitals are normal, but reminds me this can change quickly.

December 16

It's three o'clock in the morning, and Acy's voice wakes me. With garbled speech, he manages to say, "I'm dying."

I move over by his side. His eyes are closed as I hold his hand. I squeeze his hand, and his eyes open. I tell him, "I love you, sweetie."

His mouth moves, but no words come forth. He struggles so hard to talk, he pulls himself up from the bed. Finally, I hear a whisper. "I love you too."

Then he collapses backward onto the bed. He regains his strength and says, "I'm hungry."

I feed him, and he's able to eat a few bites of ice cream, and drinks a sip of water.

He's quiet, and his eyes are closed. I think he's asleep. I decide to get some shut-eye.

I'm awakened in time to see him walk down the hallway and enter the bathroom. He pees and returns to his bed.

It's been a few hours, and he insists on going to the bathroom again. When he's ready to return to the living room, I talk him into wearing adult pull-ups, and help him back to the bed.

I hear the phone and answer it. While I'm distracted, even though the rails are raised, he manages to sit up on the side of the bed. I'm told if I raise the foot of the bed, he can't crawl out. I keep raising it higher, but he keeps crawling out. He uses his feet and legs to pull himself upward on the foot of the bed. When he's high enough, he grabs the rails and turns himself around.

He continues to struggle throughout the day, so I lower the foot of the bed and help him sit up. I leave the rail up and stand in front of him in case he needs support. It's been days since he's had a meal, and I'm worried he may faint. He says, "Now, get the hell out of my way!"

He can't help it. It's Alzheimer's. Maybe laced with a little stubbornness, maybe a lot of stubbornness. I refuse to move. He pushes against me, but his arms go limp, and he lies back down.

December 17

There are only the two of us here today. We're in the midst of back-to-back snowstorms. The snow paralyzes the traffic, and road crews are working on the roads. Acy's nurse skids off the road and into the ditch, and her husband rescues her.

I feel the need to have someone here with me. I start up the computer and find my way to TheAlzheimerSpouse.com. I find my online friends ready to hold my hand through cyberspace. They comfort and encourage me. There is always someone here if I need to talk. I'm not alone.

Acy no longer consumes food, but today he drinks one-half a teaspoon of water at a time. It keeps his mouth moistened.

He's fighting to get up with all he's got. He pulls himself up by the rails and falls back. He rests for a while, then I hear him stir. He appears to be talking to himself. "I hurt all over. Where's my gun?"

Some of this could be withdrawal from the medicine he takes for PTSD. He can't swallow, so there's no way for him take it now.

December 18

I resolve to try one more test. I ask Bessie to stay with him, and I travel to Wendy's one last time for a Frosty. I return, and Acy's eyes light up when he sees the Frosty. I place half a spoonful in his mouth, but it slides back out. I give him half a teaspoon of water, and it dribbles out. He's lost all ability to swallow.

It's time to change his adult pull-ups, and he resists. He refuses to let me roll him. When I try, he clutches the rails and hangs on with everything he's got. I put my arm under his legs and lift, but he pushes his legs back down.

"Acy, I need to get these wet clothes off you." Once again, I put my arm under his legs, and he stiffens. I put my hands under his knees. "Acy, bend your knees."

I glance at his face. He's got his, "I'm not going to let a woman tell me what to do," look on. I try again, but he's stiffer than the bed railing he holds on to. I'm at my wits' end. Out of frustration, I tell him, "If you don't bend your legs, I'm going to break them."

He decides not to call my bluff and relaxes his legs. Now I'm able to change him.

I talk to the nurse, and she tells me, "This is normal. Some will fight till they are too weak to resist. Then it'll get easier."

That would be a first. He hasn't made any stage easy in this journey. I tell her, "I hate Alzheimer's."

December 19

Bessie stops by and helps me bathe Acy and change his bedding. I walk her to the door, and we step outside to talk. She says she will help me each day. She leaves, and I return to the living room. He's not in his bed. My eyes scan the room. There he sits in his wheelchair.

December 20

I'm in the kitchen feeding the cats, and decide to check on Acy. I gasp. *He's gone! How did he get out of bed? Where is he?* I hurry down the hall and spot him. He's made it to the bathroom. He stands over the toilet and pees. I know his determination keeps him going, and I admire him for it, but still I'm not sure this is a good idea.

The hospice nurse keeps her appointed visit. I update her on Acy. From across the room, we hear, "Ted Turner."

I look at Acy, and he's watching Ted Turner on the TV. The nurse thinks he was reading the bottom of the screen. I'm of a different opinion. Seldom has Acy failed to recognize a face. He's always admired Ted Turner. Is it possible he put name to face? I suspect this is what he did.

The nurse calls the doctor and explains that I'm having trouble keeping Acy in bed. She calls in a prescription for Ativan to give him. She says to put it in his rectum, that it works the same way as taking it orally. I can't leave him alone, so the pharmacist brings it to me. The Ativan works, and now he's calmer.

Acy develops a problem with congestion in his airway. He can't cough it up, and it rattles as he tries to breathe. It's late evening, but my instructions from hospice are to call them day or night if we need them. I call for assistance, and I'm told there's no one available to help me. The representative says I should call back the next day. I spend the rest of the night by Acy's side.

December 21
It's morning, and I call hospice at 8:00 a.m. I explain Acy's problem to the receptionist. I ask her for a pump to suck out the congestion. She says there's no way they can get a pump here anytime soon. She has no idea when they can get here because it's a two-hour drive. That being the case, I say I will call an ambulance to take him to the hospital. She reminds me he'll lose his hospice if I do that.

I say, "That's fine. I'm firing you anyway."

I call the ambulance, and they rush him to the hospital. I update the doctor on the circumstances surrounding Acy's problem, and the ambulance attendants agree the congestion is making him struggle for air. The doctor instructs someone to clear his throat.

He asks, "Do you want me to intercede and run tests."

"No. All I want to do is keep him comfortable," I say. "When I agreed to use hospice, I was told their purpose was to make him comfortable. They said they would be available to us around the clock. Since they don't appear to be equipped for the job, I no longer have a use for them." I inform the doctor, "I've used the pump before. I used one on my mother when she was dying from lung cancer. I would appreciate it if you would write me a prescription for one, and I'll get it filled at the medical supplies store on the way home."

The doctor leaves for a time and then returns. He informs me that two people from hospice are in the hospital. He advises me, that since I only want Acy made comfortable, maybe I should reconsider and work things out with them. He tells me they are willing. I look over at Acy, move in closer to him, and hold his hand. I agree to talk with them.

The two ladies from hospice enter the room. I don't feel this should be discussed in front of Acy. He doesn't talk or respond, but he stills hears and understands. They ask a hospital staff member to find a room for us.

They ask me to explain what happened. I tell them the events that led to this hospital visit. They apologize, and say there has been a communication breakdown. I'm assured they will investigate to find the problem.

Acy returns home in an ambulance, and I follow in the SUV. Shortly after, his nurse drops by, and someone shows up with a pump. I'm instructed on how to use it. They depart, and the aide arrives and gives him his bath. Before she leaves, she says to call her if I need her tomorrow.

December 22

I rise early to check on Acy. He lies quietly, and his eyes shut out the world.

Around noon, he rouses from his slumber. "Dorothy!" he yells. "Come here!"

"What's wrong?" I ask.

"I need to piss."

"It's OK. Go ahead and pee."

"Nooo!"

My mind reels. I can't bear to rob him of his dignity. Pride is all he has left. I find some pads I bought to line his underwear.

"OK. Wait just a minute."

"Hurry!"

I take a pad and wrap it around his penis. "OK. I've fixed it so you can pee in the pad."

He pees, and my little invention works. This goes on all afternoon, and not once does he get his pull-ups wet. By evening, he's peed out.

Bessie stops by and stays with him so I can leave the house for a while. I return, and she sits with us until nightfall. After she leaves, I take a nap. I wake and sit by Acy's side.

December 23

It's now midnight. It's December 23, 2010. I watch while Acy's breathing slows. As he slips into unconsciousness, he says in a low, soft voice, "Let's go."

At some point, I know he will have to make this trip alone. I can't really tell him it's OK to die. He would see that as treason. Part of me longs to speak his name and tell him one last time that I love him. The other part is afraid he might start struggling again. I sit beside him and hold his hand. I squeeze it to send him a message of love.

At 12:30 a.m., I watch him draw his last breath. He doesn't go alone. He takes my heart with him.

I spend some private time with him to tell him good-bye. Then I call hospice. I call Bessie, and she returns to stay with me.

Shortly after hospice notifies them, his friends, who work at the funeral home arrive. One of them has the job of checking to see if he's breathing. He hesitates and says, "You know, I dread doing this. I expect him to sit up and ask me what the hell I'm doing."

After the exam, they stay awhile, and we reminisce.

It's time for them to go. It helps to know he's leaving with friends. I ask them to wait, and I give him one last kiss on the cheek. This is the last time I will ever see him.

Arrangements

His wishes were to be cremated without funeral services. I prearranged plans with the funeral home. They handle the cremation. They tell me I don't need an urn. The box from the crematory will do.

A week later, I buy niches at the cemetery. I stop by the funeral home to pick up his ashes, but they don't have them. They bring them to me the next day.

I soon realize the box won't do. It's only a cardboard box. I buy an urn I feel would meet Acy's approval. The funeral home will transfer the ashes into the urn. It seems like such a personal thing to do, I decide to do it myself. I've read, that in the Old World, this was a tradition done as part of closure. When I open the box, I find a small certificate that says he was cremated December 25, 2010.

His ashes remain at home for several months as he requested. I need to know that if anything happens to me, Acy's ashes will be safe in his final resting place. Madge, from hospice, offers to go with me, but I feel the need for privacy.

I carry his ashes to the car and place them in the seat that carried him through many travels, including trips to his beloved Wendy's. I escort his ashes to the cemetery. I place them in his niche and say farewell one last time. I turn my back and walk toward the door. I hear the cemetery workers replace the cover. I walk down the aisle with one thought in mind. *He no longer needs me.*

As I drive toward an uncertain future, I think, *Maybe Madge was right. Maybe I should compile my experiences as a caregiver for a dementia patient.*